It's Never So Bad That It Can't Get Worse!

Dr. Gary Vonk

Illustrations by Duane M. Abel

Copyright © 2021

All Rights Reserved

ISBN: 978-1-7369996-1-5

Dedication

I dedicate this book to my children,

Garrett, Christine, and Stephen

who have provided me with unequalled inspiration for going forward and tackling the world!

They too have shared in this journey.

Special thanks also to Robi, my wife, who shares with me the joy of doing.

Contents

Introduction 6

Chapter 1   Oh No, I'm in Charge 12

Chapter 2   Right Sizing Is Right If You Are Left 21

Chapter 3   What's your GSI? 31

Chapter 4   Do Something You're Proud of 39

Chapter 5   Dinosaurs Ate the Low-Hanging Fruit 48

Chapter 6   Even If You Are on the Right Track, You Will Get Run Over If You Just Sit There! 62

Chapter 7   How Many of Us Have Been Thanked Too Much? 70

Chapter 8   Every Manager Teaches Us Something 77

Chapter 9   *Dress* for The Job You Want 84

Chapter 10   First Remember What Got You Here, Then Think about Where You Are Going 92

Chapter 11   Members of the Ancient Tribes Who Did Not Get Along, Got Eaten! 100

Chapter 12   Helping Others Help You 107

Chapter 13   The Environment Drives Success: It Is up to You 115

Chapter 14   Trust and Be Trusted! 122

Chapter 15   I Learn More When I Listen Then When I Talk 130

Chapter 16   Develop an Entrepreneurial Mindset 136

Chapter 17   Putting it All Together - Ok, so now what do I do? 145

Introduction

I have been blessed with quite a number of years in the corporate world. Of course, it has its ups and downs but most importantly, during those years, I realized that so often the outcome was up to me. There are times when you feel like you are on making great progress and you are on top of the world. There are also times when you feel that there is no point in putting your heart and soul into the daily struggles. I am hoping this book might provide a little guidance on some of the lessons learned and how to possibly develop a balance in your work-life, which will help you stay focused on the goals ahead. These lessons don't simply translate into the corporate world, as there are plenty of lessons and examples that you can apply to both your professional and personal lives. The point is to constantly re-evaluate and look for strategies that will give you the desired outcome and help guide you on your path through life. Not all of these scenarios will apply to your work or life, as we are all faced with many unforeseen opportunities. However, I hope that some will resonate and that you might find some choices that will assist you in your journey.

With anything we undertake, there are times when the plans just don't work out. But the real keys to developing winning strategies, is when things don't work out, you go back and try again. We all must understand that we are the agents of change in our own lives, and often the lives of others, and we need to take the appropriate steps to develop solutions in our personal and professional lives. We really need to understand that **we** can be the ones to transform the world. Often times our efforts will serve to transform the lives of others and perhaps our efforts will ripple throughout the organization. Although, our efforts may not change the world, they can change us all, of that I am certain.

So, what makes me, Gary Vonk, such an expert on talking about these things? Well, I spent thirty (30) years in management and senior management positions. This means that I was either the CEO or the VP of those companies. I started out in retailing in 1968, which seems like a lifetime ago. But I started at the bottom and worked my way upward. That is an important lesson to remember. It doesn't matter where you start. Most of us are conditioned to believe that we need to start in a position of responsibility or a good starting salary to get somewhere quickly. Looking too far ahead may prevent us from seeing exactly what is in front of us and the problems that we can solve. If we don't think this way, we may end up blocking our chances of getting to some good place. I am here to let you know that it is perfectly acceptable to start at the bottom and work your way to the top. In the process, there is lot's to be learned.

I have touched many business sectors, from multinationals to startups, from jewelry stores to real estate. I believe I had seen more than most typical workers, but I still wanted to grow. So, I decided to concentrate on academics, providing me an opportunity to give back. Yes, I had all of this real-life knowledge and experience that proved invaluable, time and time again, but I felt like going back to school could bring out the teacher in me. I had not stepped foot into academics since I graduated from college, until I had this burning desire to learn something new in a wholly new environment. I enrolled in a university in Florida and got my master's degree. Then, I moved on to get a doctorate and also served as the president of a local university campus.

Now, I can honestly say that it is not just the corporate world that I am familiar with, although unarguably that is the area in which I have much experience. But it is very important to understand that learning is an important part of the journey and it never stops. Venturing into other areas, seeking additional knowledge, and acquiring new skill sets, will always add to your success.

One of the lessons I have learned in my career is always to look toward the *opportunity* side of things. You see, no matter how bad we think we have it, the idea is that things can always get worse. A simple example: let's assume that you had the absolute worst day at work. You leave your office, cursing and swearing, and think that things just could not get any worse. You throw your stuff in the car and settle into the driver's seat. You are too busy mulling over the day's events and don't see that there is a person crossing behind your car. You just put your car in reverse and go. You hear a thud. You look around and see someone on the ground. Your heart is exploding, and you are scared like never before.

The point of this brief example is to illustrate that things are not always as bad as we think. There is always a situation that can make matters worse. So, look at your problems in a new light and try to address them instead of thinking that there is no way out of it. There always will be a way. You just need to expand your outlook on the horizon of life. The rest will follow. This is one lesson I encourage you to embrace.

Why Am I Writing This Book?

There are times when I feel that we are missing the opportunity to share with each other because we are so busy. Some of the things that we miss out on are how to thank people, how to build teams, and how to interact with others. These might be considered the little things, but trust me, they are not. These are invaluable skills that are needed. These are day-to-day strategies that will help us to achieve short and long-term goals in life.

My intention is to share my experiences with you so that you can visualize them and apply them in your life. It may serve as a supplemental guide on your journey. Oftentimes, I feel that people are not willing to share their techniques and skills, especially in the corporate world. That is one mistake many people make. I believe that it is only by helping each other and building strong teams that we can fully develop. So, here in this book, you will learn about my skill set and the wisdom I discovered along the way. I am lucky to have all of these experiences and I feel even luckier to be able to pass them on to you. I hope they bring you great success, as they have for me.

What's in This Book for You?

Simply put, you might read this book and evaluate what exactly you need to do. There might be times when you are not sure what you are doing is wrong or right. This book might help to lighten that load. I expect that by going through these chapters, you will find a technique or two to increase your impact on others. You might see who you should be thanking, and maybe even, who you should be letting go to make your team a better one. And take a second to see how you can apply these things in your personal, as well as professional life. I wish you all the best on this journey! Here's to hoping that you discover ways to transform your life, the lives of others, and maybe even the world!

Summer 2020 UPDATE

So, in a manner supportive of the title of this book, I will share a little story to reinforce the daily challenge of <u>It's Never So Bad That It Can't Get Worse</u> *which occurred while I was finalizing this book.*

Heading home from work one weekend day this past Summer, I encountered a large group of cyclists essentially blocking the traffic lanes on the way to my residence. After avoiding oncoming traffic, a number of times, I elected to pass this group in order to get to my residence. Low and behold two of those bikers followed me onto my private property and accosted me as I was getting out of my car. At the time I was putting my concealed carry into my pocket and my briefcase in hand. They managed to exhibit extraordinary road rage and threatened me multiple times. After a twenty-minute emotional exchange recorded on their GoPros, the bikers left with the final salvo of "We have guns and know where you live!". Shaken, I retreated to my residence. Later that week I get a call from my boss that the TV station is carrying a story on the incident and wanted a statement from me. The papers followed and it went completely viral. Although the newspaper article mostly exonerated me, the internet is forever. And now a search of my name yield this "story" for all to share. Even when it is unrelated to the facts. I mention this as I know the story will remain forever and that a purchaser of this book, might wonder about the incident when searching my name. Well, so be it. This type of incident clearly illustrates the concept of the title of this book. Take a long day tackling the COVID-19 risks and requirements and then head home late only to encounter an event that makes the day even worse. Hopefully a lesson learned and reinforcement of the premise I share with you today.

Chapter 1
Oh No, I'm in Charge

"Before you are a leader, success is all about growing yourself. When you become a leader, success is all about growing others." —Jack Welch

Let's suppose that you are working in a corporation and one day you are called into the CEO's office. You hurry, wondering what is going on. Your stomach is in knots, anticipating what is going to happen. Your mind is thinking about the things that you have done. Perhaps you have done something wrong, which is why you are being summoned so suddenly. You get there and find out that your manager is being transferred to another unit and the new manager is...you. You...are now in charge! At first, you feel elated that your efforts are finally being recognized. The long hours that you put in the office were not going unnoticed. But then, you feel weird. You start to get panicky. You wonder if you are cut out for this job.

Suddenly, you feel there is a mountain on your back, and you have no control over how things will turn out. The panic starts to grow, and you cannot think straight. You wonder what steps you can take to assume the responsibility of the new position.

Well, instead of sitting and worrying about things that may or may not happen, you need to assess the situation and circumstances, and do the best you can with the information you have. Tackle the things that you can get your arms around, and sometimes worry in the dark if the other things will happen or not. But never let those thoughts impact on the execution of what needs to be done on the day-to-day basis. That's what smart people do. So, when in charge, the following are some of the things that you can do to overcome the bouts of panic and prove yourself successful.

Identify and Affirm Your Values and Core Commitment

Before, during, and after leadership transition, are good moments to reflect on the values and core commitments of leadership. You should keep an open mind about the opportunities and challenges that you will most likely encounter on your path, because there are some strategies that you can implement.

- Keep going back to your basic values. Make sure they are visible. Try writing them on a post-it note; paste them on your computer screen or windshield, anywhere you can see them frequently. This will be a constant reminder of your values and keep you motivated.

- You can also keep a journal and reflect on the things that are emerging in the work life. There is a possibility that some of these things are messed up because of the transition. It could be that things are too challenging for you. Take the time to know where you are before you move forward.

- Also, take the time to understand how your values may change, given this new role. Perhaps they need to be redefined because of the new commitment that you are facing. Maybe, consult with other people, those who have been through this change, as well.

Understand That in Order to Move Forward, We Have to Let Go of Our Past

According to the book, *The Real Reason People Won't Change* by Lisa Lahey and Robert Kegan, sometimes people refuse to transition because of the underlying assumption they have about the people around them or the assumptions those people are making of them. To counter this, you need to ask yourself what you are facing and what makes you feel so resistant to change. Ask yourself what would happen if you were to say yes. Ask what matters and what will you gain from this situation. Are you able to feel grateful for what happened and for what is going to come? There are times when you feel that handling leadership is less about letting go and moving on and more about finding comfort with the way things are changing. There are moments when we have eagerly waited for change, but when it finally arrived, it was slower than we wanted. You have to know where the problem lies. Maybe the change itself is not the problem; maybe it is the pace of change that is proving to be a problem for you. For instance, in the above example, even if you have accepted the change, those around you may have not, which will make the pace slower. But you have to be patient about it and work to find daily opportunities.

Distinguish between Fear and Fact

Most of us have this problem. We end up fearing things that may never be realized. I remember when I was going through a merger and a colleague of mine called me in Oklahoma from California, saying there was a terrible problem. He told me he had messed up. He offered to resign once the problem was fixed because it was so bad, it might affect the merger transaction. I told him to calm down, get on the next plane, and we'll figure this out together. We sat together and four or five days later, we presented the information to the acquiring company and everything went smoothly. The transaction closed and the merger happened successfully. The lesson learned is that an organization can be built to tackle any challenge, so long as the team believes it can. Critical to the success of this merger was the team's reaction to the crisis which served to resolve the problem and achieve the ultimate objective.

Now picture this. You get an email close to 5 p.m. on Friday and you are still a newly minted leader. A colleague reports that the funding for a program is about to be cut, and you, barely into the new job, want to save it. Before you weigh in, you need to ask yourself what the facts are. Know that in stressful times, rumors are high and the information you receive might be overblown, manipulated, or even just tweaked to add fuel to the fire. Leadership is all about navigating through uncertainty. This means dealing with the rumors that often come flying your way instead of jumping on the bandwagon and without dissecting facts from fears. Take the time to investigate what is happening and then take steps to overcome the situation. Remember, what sometimes looks like the end of the world is just another chapter.

Be Professional

The norms that guide our work lives should be pretty clear and help us pave our path. However, things are not always that easy. The twists and turns sometimes make it more difficult to know how to act and which direction to take. The one thing that you can do to counter that is to take a piece of paper and write down how three of your closest colleagues would describe you. Ask yourself who you show up as most of the time and how you need to change according to the situation in front of you. Leaders self-assess all the time. It helps keep them grounded in their role and provides personal feedback. Go over your to-do list and see where your energy must be applied.

Deal with Emotions

Being a leader means taking care of so many things that come your way. It means always being alert about the different situations that you may be dragged into. With this pressure in mind, it can be a bit difficult to keep your values at the forefront and embrace the change. Focus on the facts and bring your best professional self to work every single day. So, if you are stressed and unable to be this person, stop and "take a deep breath." As overrated as it sounds, there is truth in the statement. If you were to look at the research, you would find that there is so much support in the power of breathing. It helps to defuse difficult situations, in addition to conversations and emotions. We also have apps that guide us through this purpose. They're free, so you can easily download and listen to them. A leader with a clear head is critical.

Changes in the Job/Role

Leaders need to transform multiple times and take on multiple roles in the process. They begin with managing themselves, managing others, and managing other managers. There is also the element of functional management, business leadership, as well as group leadership. At each level, the individual has to acquire new skills and competencies. The skills that the leader has used in the previous role might not be applicable in the next role. Moreover, the leader grows and adapts to the job and this may cause restructuring, reorganization, as well as mergers and acquisitions. As the leader grows and develops, they have to look for new ways to improve things. This adds value to the performance and the role of the leader. A leader needs to build these roles in order to move ahead. Failure to do so will mean that the individual will have no control over themselves or their team. Pretty soon, they will be forced out of their role.

You Are Promoted for a Reason

When people are thrust forward in this role of leadership, they sometimes get panicky to the point that they are unable to think clearly or function properly. Previously, when they could handle just about every pressure that the company was throwing at them, they now cannot even see two feet ahead. Needless to say, this builds even more pressure, and the first thought of the new leader is that they have made a mistake, they are not cut out for this type of work, and therefore, they need to step away. When these thoughts swirl in your mind, calm down and relax. Think about who you are and why leadership has picked you to fill in the new position. There must be something your superiors saw in you as the reasons that they decided to put you in charge. You just need to concentrate on that and bring those abilities forward. If you are truly confused about what they saw in you, you always have the option of going to those in power and ask. Use the skills that your wiser and smarter superiors recognized, those skills that would make you a great leader. Another option, if your superiors are not available, is speak with your colleagues. Ask them why they think you have been chosen. The chances are they will be able to highlight the qualities in you that you have not seen in yourself. Make these qualities your strength and use them to move forward, achieving one goal after another. It is not about age and experience. It has to do more with skills. Most often, people think that they cannot become leaders until they have achieved a certain level of experience. I am here to tell you that this is not the case.

I became a VP for an international corporation at the age of 38. At the time, that was a relatively young age to be in such a position, but I managed it. I not only managed it, I also thrived in that setting. This is why I am ensuring you that you have the inherent skills to be successful. Another mistake people make, is that they look for ways to get individual credit for a situation. That cannot work most of the time and it is why it should not be your focus. The credit that your team and your leadership get will be far more rewarding. Look for ways to be successful and the credit will automatically come to you. Focus on getting the results for your company and the success will follow. As a leader, when you work hard, develop people to the degree that they achieve; guess who is also successful along the way? –Y.O.U.

Embrace the Position

You have been promoted. You look at yourself in a mirror and say, "What the heck did I do to deserve this? How did I do that?" Remember, it is all about embracing your personal landscape. Know that you have been chosen for a reason. Once you have figured out what the reason is, you will be able to get to the place where you want to be. The best thing to do is to take everything in stride. Yes, you will face obstacles, but when does anyone not face obstacles? Personal growth comes from encountering difficulties. Think about the time when you started in the company. Maybe the week before you started your new job or your first job, you were worried. You did not know if you were going to last there for a week, let alone a month. But you made it through, despite having to jump high hurdles along the way. You did it because you have it in you to take on the problems and find solutions. If you don't take on the new role, you might regret it for the rest of your life. Being scared is not the solution, tackling it head-on is. Even if you take on the role and decide to step back later, at least you will have had the experience. Next time, when you have the chance to become a leader, you will know what to do. You will learn from the mistakes and do better next time. In this way, you can progress even more. The one important thing to remember is that it is all within you. You need to be the one to unleash the potential. Yes, the boss saw the abilities in you, but it is up to you to nurture and bring them forward, so when you are the one who is in charge you can foster this belief in others.

<u>Something to remember:</u>

Tackle the things that you can get your arms around, and sometimes worry in the dark if the other things will happen

or not, but never let those thoughts impact on the execution of what needs to be done on the day-to-day basis.

Chapter 2
Right Sizing Is Right If You Are Left

"When written in Chinese, the word crisis is composed of two characters -- one represents danger, and the other represents opportunity." John F. Kennedy

We live in a very uncertain time. At every step of our journey, we are expected to navigate uncertainty. Employees are also supposed to be on their toes all the time. However, it was not always like this. For those who have worked in the 80s and 90s, things were not so complex. You would go to work, do the job you were supposed to do, and then leave. You had a stable job, for the most part. Even if there was some level of uncertainty you could navigate it fairly easily. Now things are not as simple. There is so much uncertainty prevailing that leaders and employees have to take a new approach. Take a look at the post-coronavirus world. It is as if the whole world had changed overnight. So many businesses had to go digital within a couple of hours. There were plenty more that had to lay off their employees. This brings me to my main point - downsizing.

The Need for Downsizing

Most of us know what downsizing means. But for the sake of clarity, let me define downsizing as when a company terminates multiple employees at the same time to save money. It is important to remember, it is not done because the employees have a behavior problem, it is done because of the changes in the organization. The aim is to reduce headcount in any way possible. This does not mean direct firing. Employees have the option to step down voluntarily. However, in extreme cases, they are laid off.

So why does this happen, you may wonder. Here are just some of the reasons why.

Recession

Perhaps the most common reason is because of changes in the economy. Poor economic conditions give rise to failing businesses. As they are unable to cope with the fall in profits and rises in costs, they look to other ways to make ends meet. This comes in the form of layoffs. Salaries are cut to save expenses and maintain profitability.

Merger

The second most common reason is when two companies are merged, or one company takes over another. New management comes in and the old management is let go. New and more skilled employees are sometimes preferred, which means letting go of the previous ones. Again, this has nothing to do with the credibility of the employee. It's just that an entire organization faces restructuring and with it, there are changes that cannot be avoided.

Industry Decline

Industries decline and new ones arise. With the advent of technology, so many firms have become obsolete. As a result, there are plenty of skills that have become outdated. New people need to be hired in order to change the direction of the industry. These are people who are trained in the relevant field. The other employees who are not up to the mark are let go.

Competition

Organizations constantly compete. They do whatever they can to be in the lead. When one organization downsizes its employees, other organizations feel the need to do the same. This helps them cut costs and raise their profit level.

A Leader's Role

There are many employees who are laid off every year, especially when the company is downsizing. In 2017, the top 12 employers conducted layoffs which reduced the workforce of more than 47,000 employees. Try as we might, downsizing is now an inevitable part of the corporate culture. While downsizing varies from one company to another, there is no industry that is exempt from it. There is also no discrimination between public and private companies as both lay off employees. That is the reality of the business world.

Layoffs are not for just one group of people, but they affect all the employees regardless of their class. They affect every area of an organization from executive leadership to entry-level positions. Managers are more affected by the downsizing since they are responsible for leading the organization during these changes. They are the ones who have to deal with the aftermath of those changes. It is not easy to do that, and the manager has to develop the skills and take appropriate action. The employees always resist the notion. This is a fact.

I remember working in an automobile industry where I once decided to gather all the managers in one room and address them. As they sat around the table, I looked at them and said, "You guys are more important today than you were yesterday."

They looked at me and asked in confusion, "Why did you say that?"

My honest reply was that I did not know anything about the industry. That I had never been in the situation before. I explained to them I was not only there to teach them, but also to learn. I asked them to present to me, what they see as an opportunity.

We are not successful until we help someone succeed as well. About sixty days later, we were back in the same room. "Ok, everybody, here is my decision. Here is what we need to do. We need to cut down half of our staff." I apparently caught their attention.

The very next moment, still sitting around the table, they blurted in unison, "Oh my gosh, we will never survive. You can't be serious. You can't do that." Anxiety permeated the room for the next few minutes.

I finally spoke again, "Ok, here is what we can do. We can cut 50% of the staff and drive this company successfully or cut 100% and the whole thing disappears. What do you guys want to do? Take some time to think about it, talk among yourselves, and I'll be back in a while."

When I returned to the room, their response was immediate, "I think we can do it."

The idea is that we need to let employees figure out what works best, instead of hijacking the whole operation. In my case, they came to the understanding that they were better off with half the workforce.

Here are a few tips for the leader to diligently perform their role.

Stay Informed

You need to be informed about the changes in the business. Rumors do reach the ears of the employees and they will come to ask you about them. But you cannot tell them what you do not know. You also need to prepare them, which cannot happen if you are unclear about what is happening around you. Yes, there will be limited information sometimes, but you have to be the one to extract all the information. In doing so, ask questions and then speak up on behalf of your team. Then, give them the full information, not bits and pieces. In the process, you will earn their respect and make navigation easier for them.

Be Transparent

Authenticity is vital, especially in times of downsizing. It is needed to reassure employees who are already in a state of panic. You have to make sure that the employees do their best by sharing information as soon as it is received. Timely communication adds more value than complete information. It is okay to let your employees know that you do not have all the answers to their questions but that you will keep them updated as soon as you are informed. Doing this will help you bind the team together. If there is no transparency, employees can assume that you are withholding information which will only add to their fears.

Avoid Rumors

As I mentioned earlier, there will be rumors that reach your employees' ears. They are more likely to occur during layoffs than at any other time in the company's operations. This will create unnecessary panic in the workplace. To prevent it from happening, you need to address the rumors at the start. Give information when it comes and prevent bad information from circulating.

Focus on the Job

Employees do not want to worry about job security. They just want to do their jobs. You need to help the team focus on the mission and enable them to do their best. Unify employees by getting them through day-to-day activities. Reassign duties fairly so that no one is overburdened.

Emphasize Opportunities

Talk to the employees and tell them that the downsizing is not always the result of financial trouble. It can be a part of the strategic plan to make operations more efficient so that the company can grow. Encourage your team to reinvent themselves by challenging the status quo and breaking out of *this is how we always did it* mentality. You may also have to hire people externally to achieve the needed goals. Do not be hesitant to do that as it will result in more growth for the business.

Support the Company

Many managers who are torn between being loyal to their company and being loyal to their employees. It is easy to side with employees, especially when you are close to them. But the boss is the one paying your salary. Therefore, you need to align yourself with them also to keep a balance.

Survivor Syndrome

Many of us have been in a position where we have seen people being laid off. You might even have prayed that you would be one of those to survive the downsizing. However, people who do survive this direct hit find that being lucky is not necessarily good. Instead of feeling thankful and grateful, they start to feel miserable. They have to go through massive workloads while waiting to see what will happen next. This is called the "workplace survivor syndrome" and is a term coined by organizational psychologists to describe the emotional, psychological, and physical effects on an employee who remains during the company downsizing. It is hard on anyone and can prevent you from doing your work properly. So, how can you move past it? The following are some of the steps that you can take to get there.

- Give yourself time to grieve. When we work together, we form a bond with our co-workers. Saying goodbye to them

can be emotionally upsetting. It is okay to step back and breathe a little.
- Do not hold grudges against the management. Resist the urge, even if you were close to your co-workers. There is no reason to take it out on the management. They did it for the greater good.
- Ask for clarification if you are confused. Understand why it is done so that it gets easier to process.
- Avoid gossiping altogether. It only adds to the stress and anxiety that you are facing.
- Find opportunity within adversity. Take on additional work. Although it can be a stressor, it can also lead to better and newer opportunities.
- Take a mental break to reconnect with friends and family. You can also take a short trip and put some distance between yourself and the company. It is okay to do that as it will help you gain more perspective.
- Cut yourself some slack but don't overburden yourself with the expectation that you are the one who has to take on the burden of the company.

There will be doubts in your head. You will wonder if the company is loyal to you and your co-workers. I am here to tell you that you need to resolve these doubts. Go and talk to your manager. Sit down with them and speak to them about what is going on. They will take the time to explain to you what is taking place. They might even share some of the goals for the company. You need to resolve those feelings of doubt that exist inside you. Otherwise, your work will become tougher and you will not be able to do what is required. Take it easy on yourself. Downsizing is hard on everyone, not just those who are let go. In fact, even the top management does not want to do it but has to put the company first.

Leaders and Mental Health

Leaders have a huge role to play in the mental health of their employees. They need to have the emotional intelligence to navigate their circumstances. Emotional intelligence is the ability to manage your emotions and recognize and respond to the kind of emotional distress done to others. The best leaders are those who have been trained to understand emotions. They are well-versed in psychology courses and recognize subtle changes in their employees. Some of the skills that you can implement are:

- Understanding emotional triggers
- Giving negative feedback in a positive way
- Having excellent listening skills
- Knowing how to ask questions that will help you recognize others' strengths
- Making no self-assumptions about employees' behavior
- Communicating without judgment
- Encouraging employees by boasting about their skills and achievements
- Making time to connect with your employees
- Appreciating your employees and making sure they know you appreciate them

If anyone is having a bad day, you need to find out why. Perhaps you can give them time off so that they can focus on the problem. Do not be one of those leaders who tell their employees to leave their problems outside the door. Neither the employee nor the leader can function properly in that circumstance. Make the problems of the employees your own problems so that they are comfortable sharing their concerns. As I mentioned earlier, downsizing is so hard. Your employees are not robots who can stay detached. Work with them so that they can do better, and you will have a more productive workforce at your disposal.

Something to remember:

Emotional intelligence is the ability to manage your emotions and recognize and respond to the kind of emotional distress done to others. The best leaders are those who have been trained to understand emotions.

Chapter 3
What's your GSI?

"So, you take this group of people. And they graduate school and they get a job. They're thrust into the real world. And then in an instant, they found out they're not special. Their moms can't get them a promotion. That you get nothing for coming in last. By the way, you can't just have it because you want it. And in an instant, their entire self-image is shattered."

- Simon Sinek

Simply put, the workplace is a gathering place for ideas and emotions that allows organizations to operate. Within the scope of this theme there are varying phases of commitment among the personnel. This is often manifest in the way the team works, both individually toward their personal goals and collectively as the team endeavors to achieve the corporate objectives. I have often said that work within many organizations is much like living on a houseboat. Once it leaves the dock, we are in it together, and often times, there is no easy way out. This perspective also comes into play as leaders within the workgroup determine the level of commitment toward the goals that each member of the team demonstrates. This indicator of the team members *level of commitment* I have identified as the team members "Give a Shit Index" (GSI). We all have worked in places that have shared goals that are not necessarily shared by each team member, nor with the same level of commitment. These varying degrees of caring can have a dramatic impact on the achievement of those goals and the morale of the team that seeks to accomplish said goals. This GSI seeks to determine how much the team members, individually, are committed to the overall goals. Those with high GSIs are often team leaders who see the objectives as clearly a function of their responsibilities and their corporate roles. Those with significantly lower GSIs are often those who are unmotivated to pull their weight, or insufficiently trained to share in the objectives. These ratings can be fluid and many times engaging the lower GSI employees with produce significant results toward the goals.

Problems often develop when members of the team continue to maintain a low GSI even when provided any and all resources to achieve success. Those unmotivated team members can negatively affect the other team members and drag down the overall performance. The key to understanding this phenomenon is understanding where you fall within the GSI matrix. If yours is high and others do not seek to follow, there are only a few choices to achieving harmony in the workplace. Either you lower YOUR GSI in order to blend in with the group or you figure out how to raise their GSIs! This may be difficult but necessary for the overall team success. If this is not achievable, for a variety of reasons, then you either get used to low GSIs or find a team that matches your GSI index!

Yes, we are all trained in getting the job done at our universities. But the fact is, the real workplace is extremely different than the conventional training environment. When graduates first enter the workplace there are often serious complications and hurdles that young and new employees do not understand. A sense of comradery that they are used to in their educational life is something they should embrace in the workplace.

The workplace is often very dynamic, and employees will not survive if they must be told continuously what their jobs are. Employees are seldom replaced because they simply do not have the training to get the job done. It is generally the case that terminations come after the employee has had the opportunity to be transformed in the workplace and become part of a cohesive team dedicated to a common goal. Those who suffer inadequate GSIs will not survive in this environment, long term.

Let's be honest. It is obviously a great benefit to you, and the organization, if you have a passion for your job. The attitude that you adopt as you engage in the workplace will have significant impact on your achievements and the potential for recognition and promotions. It also impacts life-after-work as you bring home your challenges and accomplishments.

> *"A culture is strong when people work with each other, for each other. A culture is weak when people work against each other, for themselves."*
>
> *– Simon Sinek*

The 2018 Deloitte Millennial Survey[1] states that only 50% of the

---

1 https://www2.deloitte.com/global/en/pages/about-deloitte/articles/millennialsurvey.html

millennials believe that they are fulfilled solely by the money their job brings into their lives. These numbers are enough to open the eyes of anyone to the fact that the youth does not entirely believe that financial gains will be enough to continue to drive them forward in the workplace and in life. What drove Bill Gates in the workplace, as he toiled in an industry that was in the cradle long before the Microsoft launch? It was the passion he held for his work, and his commitment to the final outcome that contributed to his ultimate success. Often times, pioneers do not see the work they are engaged in as hard work at all, it is often the concurrent passion that reduces the potential downside of hard work. Pioneers need only to believe that their passion and persistence will be enough to carve their path for your future. Today, Silicon Valley is at the forefront of modern technology and Bill Gates was one of the pioneers along the way. The simple fact is personal and financial gain strategies can be an asset that one should use to its full potential.

GSI Index

"And so, millennials are wonderful, idealistic, hardworking smart kids who've just graduated school and are in their entry-level jobs and when asked "how's it going?" they say, "I think I'm going to quit." And we're like "why?" and they say, "I'm not making an impact." To which we say, "you've only been there eight months..."

- Simon Sinek

Welcome to the time when your *Give a Shit Index* matters. We live in a time, when most employees, at all levels, cannot fully comprehend the future of their own companies.

There is endless research, TED Talks, and many other content formats where the restlessness of the future generation is the focus. Yes, the tenured employees can help you understand your experiences and assist you in finding direction, but they cannot take the steps for you. It is up to you to get out of bed every day, get ready, and demonstrate your commitment to the shared goals in your organization. You need to have ingenuity, enthusiasm, and responsibility for every project that is assigned to you. There are many ways to instill passion into an individual, the most successful is achieving goals and sharing those goals with teammates. Understanding ones *Give a Shit Index* and focusing on how much you care about achieving goals is an index that workers are silently demonstrating in the execution of their daily responsibilities.

Generally, a person is eligible for promotion when they have demonstrated their abilities and capabilities to handle the needed takes of their assigned responsibilities. It is more prevalent for people to be promoted when they demonstrate how they exercise even greater commitment by going above and beyond. People who ger promotions need to show commitment and passion.

GSI Index Compatibility

Successful workplaces operate when people trust each other. Trust and belief that you want to get the job done are crucial to a business' success. You have to understand that the supervisor is trusting you with the future of the company, in many ways, as was done with him or her many years before.

The simple fact is that individuals who are trusted across the workplace are promoted more frequently. Learn the ways to earn the trust of your co-workers and employers.

Find practical coping mechanisms and ways to manage your day, proactively. A lot can happen in a day. You can be having a great day one second, and suddenly, a really big issue comes your way. This is why when you come across an issue, simplify the process by finding a solution. Look at one problem at a time and focus on finding one solution at a time. It will look overwhelming if you have five problems on your plate. But once you start finding solutions, these problems will be resolved.

GSI Index: Can-Do Spirit

The single greatest challenge an employee faces in an environment where employees demonstrate varying GSIs is that they must align with the high GSIs and seek to get the lower one's up-to-speed. There is a constant need for assessment and evaluation regarding the team's commitment. Too often low GSI team members seek to find others on the team as a means of developing comradery with similarly motivated teammates. This is one of the great challenges for the high GSI team members as they must either get the low GSIs to improve their commitment and caring attributes or find team members who can. Employees who find themselves in a perpetually low GSI workplace must then make the decision whether it is worthwhile to attempt to convert as many as possible or find a group that matches their high GSI.

Deciding to give up on changing others may lead to lowering one's own GSI. Take charge of yourself and find teammates who match your index. Those who believe in established organizational milestones that prove commitment and enthusiasm, will drive success. Your leadership will recognize these traits and victory will follow. You will also find that those low GSI teammates will also self-select themselves for other work or unemployment. It is at the core of *Giving a Shit Index* that you must try and make sure that you continuously strive for success. You must learn the joy of achieving significant and positive results. The slow process of understanding your job, until such time you are trusted to do it on your own, is a great experience. Coupled with that knowledge you learn to pave your way through the valley of patience.

Understand Fulfillment

Some members of the team have a difficult time understanding where there is value in personal fulfillment. Many in the workplace are fond of saying that they do not feel fulfilled. My statement to them usually is, explain your concept of fulfillment. They want to feel like they have contributed to the world and are a good part of the community. They also want to make an impact on the people around them. So, if you want to make an impact on the world around you, you need to learn how to engage with your world. The fulfillment you want can be achieved by becoming part of a successful team, making serious and important contributions to the overall success, and helping others to succeed along the way.

The world is evolving, and technological advancements have turned into a wild card. You can expect many technological advancements in short order and many of them will have a unique impact on the human race. These advancements just a short time ago were unforeseen and quickly became part of the everyday work environment. The random influx of these unique products into the workplace requires significant flexibility and also organizational commitment. Change is inevitable.

The real issue is understanding how the *Give a Shit Index* has power in the workplace and how understanding its impact on the team's performance can be recognized and managed. The more you engage with the people around you, the better your everyday experience will become and the more successful the business in which you operate.

Something to remember:

Take charge of yourself and find teammates who match your GSI index. Those who believe in established organizational milestones that prove commitment and enthusiasm, will drive success.

Chapter 4
Do Something You're Proud of

" If it ain't fun, don't do it." - *Jack Canfield*

I should have started with a longer quote, right? Maybe. But nothing is a more effective than people who work to their strengths. We understand the process of building a career is long and arduous. You need an immense amount of passion to be able to deliver a successful lifelong journey in only one field. By the way, I'll quote Jack Canfield several times as he has great insight into building an *attitude of gratitude*, I encourage you to buy his book, The Success Principles: How to Get from Where You Are to Where You Want to Be.

What Goes Around Comes Around

> *"Gratitude is the single most important ingredient to living a successful and fulfilled life." - Jack Canfield*

If you are proud of the way you have lived your life, you will have a sense of contentment without any need for overarching successes. *What goes around comes around* is a great cliche, because when you do something good just for the sake of it, it has an amazing feeling. And when you see the benefit of your actions on the lives of others, you feel even better about life. Your growth and potential for reaching a new horizon will enhance due to the satisfaction you receive in the process. When I would drop my kids off at school, my parting words as they exited were "Do something you are proud of." Later that the day, if I had the chance to pick them up, I would always ask them what they had done to generate pride. Their responses often led to countless discussions regarding activities that impact others and us along the way. Today, I remind professors that they are in the transformation business and cannot seek to transform their students without being transformed themselves.

Let me share another story. A long time ago, the principal of one of my kid's schools had a flat tire. My son, just a regular kid, had not run into any major issues at his high school, so had never been called to the principal's office. One day he was walking home and noticed a car with a flat tire by the side of the street. He was surprised it was the principal's car and immediately, got down to change the tire. She asked him why he was helping her out because she had not recognized him as one of the students. He told her that his Dad had taught him how to change a flat tire and he thought it was a great time to pay it forward. It was another opportunity for him to do something he was proud of.

The story also has so many other simple lessons about *do good and you will have good*. The next time she saw me she mentioned the help my son had rendered and how selfless it had been. You will decide whether you are a positive force in the history of humanity or negative, depending upon how you choose to live it every day.

Know Your Strengths

> *"Decide what you want, believe you can have it, believe you deserve it,*
>
> *and believe it's possible for you." – Jack Canfield*

The workplace allows us to try out our skills "with live ammunition". Meaning that we are creating, achieving, and implementing things that have an organizational impact and an individual impact on others. It is also where we can develop a sense of understanding of which areas we are skilled and which areas we still need to develop.

Your work and career life are very similar phenomenon. You need to like your career if you want to thrive and grow financially. You also need to develop a personal perspective that allows you to translate positive activities into your personal life. When these two are in balance, you can truly feel the impact that you are having on others and yourself. These simple ideas are here to help you grow your breadth and depth as a professional. They will prepare you for the world you will enter and help to shape your perspective to define your mission in life.

Internships Are Good

Internships are a great way to learn about a field without making a long-term commitment to the organization. Let me give you an example. An acquaintance shared this story of a nephew of his who always wanted to be a journalist. Throughout his childhood, he loved writing and was the permanent staff writer for his school, college, and then university magazine. When he was in his third year of college, he got an internship at a leading newspaper. He was over the moon and couldn't stop talking about the joy he felt. Finally, his internship started.

A week into the internship, it hit him hard; newspapers had become a dying industry. In a world where news is available at a moment's notice, he was astonished to find the editor proofreading the copy of a news article that had been online the previous night. Not only the basic format of developing news but staying relevant and ahead was also a challenge. Half the newspaper was filled with clips from other sources because who wants to read the views of local journalists? All of these simple facts made the journalism profession significantly less desirable.

This forced the question; why was he is interested in becoming a journalist? He still felt strongly about wanting to be a writer, but determined journalism was not the best avenue. A change of plans for his career was in the works. Trying the one profession he would love to achieve was a great way to understand his personal motivation. An internship can help to do just that. Ultimately, my friend's nephew went into writing and publishing. Soon the writing turned into published works, and now he is rocking the internet.

I shared this story to help you understand what you can do with your talent. Your talent and its connection with the real world are two separate issues. But no matter your passion and expertise, it will be your connections that will help you yield success! Be great at what you do and maximize your relationships with others.

The modern world can be taken in two ways—you can either be intimidated by it—or you can embrace it. The world will not stop evolving, so you must be committed to keeping up.

I Don't Have Any Passion

"I worked from 10 p.m. until 1 a.m. every night for a year to write the first

'Chicken Soup for The Soul' book." - Jack Canfield

Many individuals who start working or studying in a field, believe it will be easy because they like it. I'm not saying that is the only criteria, but it is clearly not that simple. Passion is a critical component of success as it will drive your performance, late in the game, when you really need it. Remaining passionate about your product, cause, or venture, will drive you and others to continue to fight the battle that leads toward victory. You will need to work harder than ever if you want to succeed in your chosen field. Simultaneously, you will also need to find ways to motivate your teammates to develop the same passion you have to achieve the ultimate goal. It is a daily process to encourage your team and develop a mentality that embodies this passion. Passion alone will not deliver success, but it is a critical ingredient in the daily journey and must be complimented by several other attributes.

Pushing Boundaries

"Good or bad, habits always deliver results." - Jack Canfield

You need to spend many hours a day focused on working and performing well. You also need to make sure that you are pushing your boundaries and trying new ideas within your field. To become great in your field you must seek out new things to learn and understand every day. Accordingly, you will never become good at something simply by doing it repeatedly. An inquisitive mind can only increase proficiency. It will help you to generate additional ways to achieve success, perhaps shorten processes, and develop partnership within your field.

My first jobs in retailing, nearly 50 years ago, was a cashier at a large chain store where I became very good at ringing up merchandise. I remember how I always wanted to learn more and do more within the store. Over time, I became department manager, then assistant store manager, and then store manager. Along the way, I continued to learn, not simply what it took to achieve the necessary job skills, but to look beyond to that next rung in the ladder. The greatest lesson learned; be great at what you do but always understand what it takes to rise to the next great challenge. Ultimately, my inquisitiveness within the retail climate allowed me to move up the executive ranks the office of president. Be good at what you do and grow every day... is something I cannot repeat enough!

Don't Ignore Your Passion

"One individual can begin a movement that turns the tide of history." - Jack Canfield

There is a balance to doing what you love. You need to understand your field of passion early and pursue it as deeply as you can. Many people may romanticize about becoming a *banker or finance person,* but they do not understand what it takes to achieve that position. Becoming a financial analyst is challenging, trust me, I know firsthand. It requires great commitment, but it can provide the foundation for so much more. Earning an MBA is great if you want to be a businessperson but what you do with it should be more important than it was to achieve it in the first place. It is important to know what the degree is preparing you for before you toil the MBA journey. The best course of action for starting any successful career is to ask yourself; what are you good at? Then, will your degree lead you to success?

Whatever field you venture into, it must be something you enjoy. One of the great challenges, is as you educate yourself, your passions may change and your alternatives may vary as you embark on the journey. It might seem that you would be better suited for a field you choose because you would stay focused in work you like. The real rule here is be focused but flexible as you close in on your goal.

How will you know if a field is not right for you? That is a common question. Here is a simple test. Does the potential for achieving success within your chosen endeavor, drive you to think of ways to achieve during your off hours? While you are resting, or sleeping are you strategizing? Do you look for ways to learn more about successful people in your given field? If the answers to those questions are yes... then it sounds like a good fit.

Many times, a person develops an interest at an early age. Particularly in high school, young minds are exposed to many things, which they find interesting, challenging, and worth investigating. Those early inquisitive stages are sometimes what drives college students to seek degrees in these areas. Often their great ideas developed during those informative years as they casually learned more and more about their targeted field. eGames and engineering are two that come to mind as we move into the next millennium. We often underestimate that the high school environment can foster this inquisitive nature. Identifying those with this focus when they enter college can yield great success for both the students and their instructors. Exposing yourself early to areas of interests and investigating them fully are the best ways to help you understand your career options and how to make the best choices.

Caution: The one inescapable point is that high school is a time for you to enjoy. Make sure you are not spending all of your time on activities that do not build your character or allow you to focus on overemphasizing the *popularity phenomenon*. Little will be achieved if being on the "most likely to be…" list does not translate into a launch of your life's journey. That being said, do not underestimate how important your circle of friends might be as you navigate the same career path, you may sometime be shoulder-to-shoulder to one of those classmates! It is always important to focus on your studies…all the while keeping your eyes on the reward.

Play the Long Game

"Clarify your purpose. What is the why behind everything you do? When we know this in life or design it is very empowering and the path is clear." - Jack Canfield

Personal soul-searching that drives your career, a novice idea indeed! But you need to understand that the world will only respond to the energy that you, and your team, put into your profession. Develop a mentality that reinforces the notion that the universe is comprised of extreme levels of energy and we are all be a part of that energy field. Understanding your position within the big picture will also allow for a clear vison of short-term victories needed to achieve long- term success. Energy yields more energy! You need to know what you plan to achieve and then you need to focus on finding a way to achieve it. A long game can sometimes be boring, and it requires you to focus and never take your eyes off the prize.

Actors sometimes say that it is hard to remember the dialog when they get to the middle of the show. In the same way, it is hard to remember the big game when the plan and strategy are being implemented. You need to assess your journey frequently, by reevaluating your course of action and determine how close you are to the critical path. You also need to make sure that the actions you take every day are moving toward your ultimate goal.

As you continue to act and focus on your goals, realize your path may be different than the one you originally thought. This is why constant reassessment is necessary. Like a sailor, who adjusts his sails in order to arrive at the final destination, these little course corrections will yield great dividends upon completion of the plan.

Something to Remember:

Passion is a critical component of success as it will drive your performance, late in the game, when you really need it.

Chapter 5
Dinosaurs Ate the Low-Hanging Fruit

"Learn as many mistakes and what not to do while your business or product is small. Don't be in such a hurry to grow your brand. Make sure that you and the market can sustain any bumps that may occur down the road." – Daymond John

The low-hanging fruit is one of the most interesting myths in the modern business world. It's roots rest on the thought that jumping into a business strategy can yield early success if you search for the easy stuff. As if things are becoming easier with passing time. Technology often makes it appear that anyone can jump into business successfully. But the truth is that business is a hard bargain to manage, with rising competition and a growing culture of outsourcing. The idea that sustainable success will be assured by tackling the easier stuff is not a long-term strategy. Yes, there are many things that mature businesses overlook as they execute their day-to-day strategies. And there are ways to take advantage of size by employing flexibility. But the low hanging fruit simply won't provide a lasting business strategy. Sustaining a business requires a certain sense of depth that successful businesses continue to utilize, even as they grow. Here is a discussion on how one can make their business come alive and they themselves can become a more resilient business owner.

What Is a Low-Hanging Fruit?

Low-hanging fruit is a solution too easy. Often times the easy stuff can be recognized as an important item for business or commerce. The items that often are taken for granted. Delivery Dudes, the Florida-based delivery service, strategized that most restaurants do not really want to own a fleet of vehicles and pay drivers to deliver their food, so it might be a good idea to invest in developing that concept. Coupled with the pandemic that rocked the world in early 2020, Delivery Dudes were able to tackle the *low hanging fruit* within this niche. Others have followed and continue to flesh out the delivery landscape, but the easy stuff is becoming less and less obvious. Now the success of these early start-ups rests with their ability to expand their offering, improve service, and reach more customers. None of these would fall into the low hanging fruit category.

This is much the case with the world's largest retailer, Amazon. The low hanging fruit served them well in the early years as they fleshed out the world's premier retail marketplace. Adding products and services continued to fuel their success as other companies tried to catch up. As the marketplace becomes more crowded it has become critical for Amazon to continue to develop in areas that may not have been in their first business plan. Those areas are often more difficult to enter and define but continue to add value to the brand and yield competitive benefits to Amazon. This is appropriate for both large and small businesses. It would seem that spending considerable time on the easy stuff might make sense in the early stages, but it will not allow you to create a sustainable model. Others will see the same opportunities and seek to intercept those same prospects. It is the tough stuff that makes your business model successful. Do the easy stuff while you develop a sustainable long-term strategy that makes it more difficult for others, whether they are big or small, to penetrate your business. If you are in the photocopy business and want to compete with FedEx/Kinkos then you had better be good at lots of other things or really great at beating them in customer service and customer contact opportunities. If you are not able to develop long-term sustainability, then you will not survive simply being "a little better" than they are.

What Easy Stuff to Avoid?

When modern entrepreneurs are getting into the market, the obvious business choices will be the most attractive. You can develop graphics on Canva, or any other online system and create an email address with Google. These are not barriers to entry, especially for others in your targeted space. If you want to operate a business, understand that you have to buy a recognizable domain, design an interactive website, and make certain that you have sufficient visual content and graphics. Obviously, that is just the start, making the business stand out and the product sustainable are the key first steps. You will also need these early as well as much more in the way of content, production, execution, and client outreach systems, before you can fully develop your business. In other words, if you are starting your business, be ready to invest in the business before you can expect to achieve any decent outcomes. You need to know who to target, develop customer outreach and client acquisition. That is often the skill that is learned early in the business development process as you fight for meaning. Much like the low hanging fruit axiom, the cheap or free stuff you can find to launch your business (email, internet, social media) will not create long term sustainability. The key to gaining business momentum is your ability to develop a good target customer acquisition plan[2]. Build your professional portfolio with tools that demonstrate your unique expertise before you start working on the venture you have planned.

Importance of Sustainable Strategy

Sustainable strategy is the difference between your business making it in the big market and the business tumbling into oblivion. If you have a great business idea, then you will need to develop a workable, long-term sustainability plan. Here are a few strategies that will assist in the development of a sustainable plan which will help you develop a more durable business.

Risk Mitigation

There are always risks that businesses must face. Understanding the perils that you may face, as you execute your plan, is critical to assessing your progress and ensuring that you continue to more toward the finish line (although there never is one!). Businesses must be structured to survive and thrive over various economic circumstances. Flexibility in the execution of

---

[2]   https://online.hbs.edu/blog/post/business-sustainability-strategies

your strategy is critical whereas you must be capable of adapting if you encounter an obstruction to progress. This requires a thorough understanding of your business and the potential challenges and how you plan on overcoming them when you encounter them. If a raw material is unavailable for your product, then what alternative is available and where? If people are not available to do the work, then where can you recruit? If the market for your product suffers downward pressure, where can you find new and exciting products or services to replace them? It is often the case that most individuals have risk tolerance limits. Not only can they not tell how and when the risks might surface, but they often have not built a plan to handle them.

The ability to handle risk is generally associated with the strength of the business. If your business is strong and customer relationship good, then encountering events that pose risk is natural. How you handle those incidents and how your customers are affected by those events, will foretell the long-term success of your business. Your risk mitigation plans must focus on ensuring that your business is healthy and thriving so that if and when the weather changes, or a car suddenly comes hurtling toward you out of nowhere, you and your business will be ready to take on the challenge.

Have Passion

Passion directed at the appropriate targets will pay long-term benefits in any business environment. Sharing your passion with the team only serves to further the enthusiastic search for success. Too often people will tell you to settle down, but the real successful people will thrive on passion for what they do, and the team achieves. You will find having a focus that does not waiver is a great gift and one that you can give to your team. Most business aspirants do not realize the business requires immense focus and often will falter without an extremely focused perspective.

Pay attention to your business and be curious about the industry and its patterns. As your company's journey plays out in front of you, you will also learn how to be more effective as you manage the ups and downs. Many entrepreneurs make the mistake thinking that what happened to other companies will not happen to them. If only you were so lucky! And once you extend your reach into the market and begin to tackle the competition, prepare for the storms that will surely hit your company. Rather than sitting in the back seat, following the actions of others, focus on learning from their experiences-both good and bad; you will find that you can avoid some of those challenges and make the most of the opportunities. It is always interesting to conduct a Strength, Weakness, Opportunity, and Threat Analysis, referred to as the SWOT analysis to identify the problems and opportunities that you will face in order to devise a plan on how to mitigate the issues and find solutions.

Focus on Sustainable Products and Services

- Why do you buy certain branded products? Often it is because they have a reputation of long-term durability. Samsung's business model depends on the concept that its products are longer lasting than the other brands that consumers find in the market. That is why it is important to focus on the development of products and services that are of high quality and long-lasting.

If you want to develop a business model for long-term client retention, then the basis of that model comes from the product or service you provide. If your service cannot hold the client, there is no point in developing the world's greatest marketing campaign. Great marketing cannot overcome poor service. Make certain your customer service team stays intimately connected with your clients. Excellent client feedback and positive client recommendation are the best way for your business to grow.

Work Together

I have said many times that team members working closely together should think as if the whole team lived on a houseboat. Once you set sail you are truly stuck with each other for good or bad. Imagine this is the case. Inevitably, it will force the team to look for ways to get along, compromise when necessary and look for solutions when others are at an impasse. This allows the team to grow exponentially, without adding personnel. We all have seen team members that find challenges in everyday duties and have frequent issues with other members. Back channel discussion usually ensues which does little to solve the problem and often fosters additional challenges. Thinking of the houseboat model will cause the team members to seek solutions, there's no place to go. Afterall, the journey will be more enjoyable if everyone gets along! Although, working together as a team can be a tough challenge. You may have disagreements, need to make connections with diverse backgrounds, and accept individuals in your permanent, everyday life. Working together and allowing for inclusive psychology can be difficult but critical to the overall success. The solution lies in adopting the right perspective. Business owners must provide the resources and allow for their effective utilization. Your employees, whether they fit in or not, will have a deep impact on your organizational success.

Key Factors of a Sustainable Strategy

Remember sustainable strategy is the difference between your business making it in the big market and the business tumbling into oblivion. Here are a few key factors that you need to understand if you are going to have a successful business.

Define Sustainability

Sustainability has different definitions depending on the leader and the organization. My definition of sustainability is that the owner of a business maintains successful financial results allowing the team to find additional revenue sources and support for the existing business. A business is sustainable, not simply because it can do the same thing over and over, but because it is always looking for greater opportunity. If a business defines sustainability with doing the same thing over and over then the next competitor can step in and replicate that model. Your competitive advantage can evaporate over-night.

Always understand that your bottom line, where you define acceptable results, will be different than other people. You need to find a way to develop a sustainability plan for your team to execute. One of the most successful ways of developing this strategy is to incorporate this line of thinking in team discussions. It is critical that the frontline employees have the ear of leadership. They will be the first to know about the good and bad experiences and will be better prepared to face the toughest questions from the customers. If you empower those front-line workers to have impact on the company strategy, then you will not be surprised as things develop.

Look for Inspiration

Entrepreneurs are often motivated by their vision of success. Whether a product or service, they are looking at ways to solve the problems or fill the needs. Very early on entrepreneurs look at the current marketplace and seek to understand those who are executing well in the space to which they are drawn. They seek to discover the ways successful people in that space are achieving results and look for potential ways to do it better. If there is no real competition, then entrepreneurs look for ways to do something that no one ever thought of accomplishing (remember… Delivery Dudes?) So emerging leaders look for key elements that his team can tackle in order to develop that sustaining strategy, discussed earlier. It cannot be a plan based on the easy/simple stuff because generally, there is not a lot of money in that type of strategy. Complexity drives competitiveness. If you do a great job in a complex business, then the barriers to entry are more substantial and the development of alternatives to your service are harder to come by. You will discover complexity builds a sustainable advantage. Therefore, before you become a competitor, learn to derive inspiration from your competition. Look at all the well-established businesses in the market. Find ways to carve out your strength and be fully in control of your brand identity.

Stagnation Is Stale

We are all comfortable with people we trust, but we cannot run a business on that motto. You need to have the best rates in the market and the best systems available. When you make a profit, make sure to refresh your vendors and company investors. Rather than trying to hold on to your financers and investors too strongly, focus on getting new blood into the business at all times. As long as you are doing your due diligence about background checks and performance evaluations, new people are the best way to grow your business.

A new team means new ideas, new concepts, and new ways to improve your business. You should have a system to make sure that you are getting in touch with changing trends and moving on with time. Your old vendors and investors should know that they have to be useful and effective if they want to stay a part of your business.

Feedback is Good

Your employees are there to advise you on the best way to accomplish goals. Leaders who unnecessarily restrict their employees' motivation can sometimes feel that their employees are not contributing to the growth of their company. Without open communication, employees will often think they do not have value and are not expected to have any original thoughts. In instances like this, both sides can feel underappreciated and perceive that the overall environment is not supportive. The result is that both sides are not going to be happy with the outcome. Leaders who encourage feedback will always be better leaders. One of the greatest challenges to inviting honest feedback is the reaction of leadership. Being defensive and upset with advice, and sometimes criticism, from employees will not serve you well as a leader in the long run. If employees face this type of negative response, they will provide you will less feedback as time goes on and potentially with less honesty. Clearly, as leader, will be missing a vital part of the business development process.

The solution to this problem is that you must listen to your employees. It can mean that you are listening to the 18-year-old kid because they are telling you how you can make the copier machine more efficient. But that kid has a right to give you feedback and you will benefit if you are willing to listen. If you give them a chance, maybe they will reduce the printing ink budget and then you will know how useful they are.

Leadership Is a Perspective

Leadership is not a job; it is a perspective. You need to be able to see the perspective of your employees, your local economy, your customers, the modern trends, and many other factors. When all of these factors come together, the leadership perspective is complete.

Here are a few steps to a good leadership skeleton that will help you develop a stronger grasp of the company you want to grow.

Be a 360-Degree Leader

You win when your team wins. No boss in the world is ever respected if they do not allow their team members to grow. Your teammates are intended to work with your company for life. They are destined to outgrow your workplace, and probably build their own company, at which time they become a strong resource within the industry. Yes, you are their mentor, but it does not change the fact that they will eventually outgrow you as a boss. Be prepared for when that day arrives. At that moment, open the door and let them go out. A good transition is a great way to make lasting relationships.

Understand the Leadership Loop

Do not cheat the process if you want people around you to trust you. For example, do not take credit for ideas that your employees develop. If you do, there won't be as many more to implement. Their trust will be broken. Always understand that an employee and leader will ultimately become a great asset. If you respect your employees, then they will also respect you. Leadership is taught to others, as they observe your style through actions. The loop is the opportunity to pay it forward and develop leaders to launch into the real world. Be part of their leadership loop and they will call you from their future position and celebrate the value you provided to their careers!

Put Others First

Leadership is about standing behind and allowing others to do their work. If you want to play in the game, then get a job. But if you want to run the game, then you will have to become the coach of your soccer field. Coaches do not play in the game. They just watch it from the sidelines. They shout at the players and tell them how to play. They do not win a trophy and barely take any credit. But they are essential to the game. You are like a coach. You are here to promote the team spirit and execute fair play. That is the only job that will truly generate long term success.

Increase Your Networking

Networking is not adding 5,000 individuals on LinkedIn and getting a LION status. Networking means you should develop a strong network of other business owners and industry experts who are there to help you understand how they achieved their goals and translate that experience as you seek to achieve your goals.

Perfection Is Overrated

Mark Zuckerberg was not perfect, and you do not have to be either. Make sure you are not set goals that are unachievable. Take the time to self-assess and see where you have achieved great things and where you have areas in need of development. This internal search will have a great impact. You will soon discover that while perfection is a nice target, the closer you get to it the farther away it moves. Find a happy balance between crazy passion to succeed and enjoying the fruits of your labor.

Something to Remember:

Focus on your business and be curious about the industry and its patterns. As your company's journey plays in front of you, you also learn how to be more effective as you manage the ups and downs.

Chapter 6

Even If You Are on the Right Track, You Will Get Run Over If You Just Sit There!

"Even if you are on the right track, you will get run over if you just sit there." - Will Rogers

How many of you remember Will Rogers? He was an American actor and great social commentator from Oklahoma. I love this quote from him; he simply explains the process of moving ahead. Growth and moving forward are significant in personal life but they are groundbreaking in your business. The mistake most business owners make, is they slow down or find satisfaction in simply making progress. A business owner must understand that they cannot slow down. If you do, you will be left behind. The modern business expands[3] or collapses.

Almost half of the small businesses do not survive in the first year

---

3   https://99firms.com/blog/small-business-statistics/

of their launch. The reason is that small businesses easily shut down and are harder to sustain. Not because of lousy ideas but generally because of poor execution or follow up. Do you want your business to survive in periods of economic collapse? If the answer is yes, then focus on expanding your small business and growing it into a medium-sized business. As the business grows, you will discover that most businesses, with more than fifty (50) employees, generally have the resources to survive. But is surviving the goal?

Of Course, but Then What?

The reason many businesses do not survive in an economic crisis or global turmoil, is because it shrinks their business to the point of inoperable. If your business is strong and large, you can adjust without completely shutting down. But if it is already small, then there is not much room for downsizing. You may have planned for a temporary interruption when significant forces prevent normal business activity, but COVID-19 proved that too many small businesses were not prepared. The truth is that setting up a business is hard and most of the business owners become exhausted well into the process. Sometimes the sense of achievement that a businessperson feels when they get to a certain point, allows them to take the foot off the gas. They become complacent and do not want to push forward and grow with the same intensity.

> *"Because I work with entrepreneurs who own businesses, I have found Doug Tatum's No Man's Land to be a really helpful body of working knowledge. It's very applicable to most businesses that have the usual problems of growing businesses - managing people, capital, markets, etc."*
>
> *- Lewis Schiff*

The simple fact is that you will need a lot of training and alternative perspectives if you want to create a successful business. You will need one trait unconditionally. You will need to have the drive. You need to be driven and you need to know that an unrelenting attitude is critical for the growth of a business. Stepping off the gas pedal is not an option.

Your Compass

Your compass for growth in your market. It is designed for you to personally track your success and to distance yourself from your peers and competitors. Do not let them catch up with you in any significant way. When it comes to your business world—be it large or small—it is important to understand that the keys to growth, is that one successful project leads to another and soon you become the market leader in your space. One factor that is critical to sustaining a long-term business plan is to have a clear understanding of your existing customer base. It is very common for existing clients to continuously evaluate their business relationships to ensure they are fully benefitting from their 'partnership'. Whether you are a direct-to-consumer business or a business-to-business partner, they will leave you for a new company, if they can improve their service, value, or timing of offering. One way to defend against this type of customer erosion is to continuously evaluate your relationship within the market and as compared to others in your space. You must keep your business model focused on innovation, expansion, and growth. Here we will discuss the ways you can continue to expand.

Review the Leakage

One key attribute that successful managers demonstrate is a clear understanding of leakage. Not specifically from the *boat is sinking 'leakage'*, but more closely focused on maintaining momentum and being watchful of areas that support the goal. Sometimes it's as simple as understanding how small costs become larger costs to your business over time. Long-term projects can develop a leak as you move from planning to implementation, the key being constant evaluation of the plan and the progress. The project execution, delivery, distribution, and many other aspects all come together to make your company earn and spend money. A regular review can help you save your finances and avoid surprises. A simple audit[4] of your business that involves the following aspects should suffice.

Quality Control

Everyone in the organization is responsible for quality control—be it answering the phone or producing and delivering. You will be challenged in growing a business if you do not have an establish quality assurance mentality. It can be very beneficial, within the manufacturing landscape, to invest in a quality assurance team that will review the produced material and adjust the product development criteria to ensure that the best products are being developed and delivered.

Supplier Performance

Of equal importance to being watchful of the delivery door, it is also critical to effectively manage receiving. Does your supplier

---

4   https://blog.fundinggates.com/2013/11/streamline-business-purchases/

deliver shipments on time and on budget? If not, what steps do you take to correct or seek alternatives? If a company does not keep an eye on the supplier's related expenses, they will lose money and momentum.

Inventory Management

If your business involves inventory of any kind, inventory management is a significant way for a company to grow its share. If you have excess products resting in your warehouse, you are officially not using your company's assets to their full capacity. Always find a way to work as best you can with *Just-In-Time* delivery criteria.

Customer Loyalty Programs

Yes, every company should have a customer loyalty program. Effectively managing your customer relationships will pay dividends long term. Remembering that the customer is part of your company assets requires you, as the leader, to remain in contact with all of your customers. One of the great challenges I faced in one of the companies I managed was that the customers were attached to the salespeople, and when the salesperson left, the customers went with them to another vendor. This can cause a rapid deterioration of your customer base. Make every customer that is being serviced by a salesperson loyal to your company. Insert yourself into the process as frequently as necessary to ensure the customer loyalty is for the company and the salesperson, in that order. If your goal is to have a loyal customer base, your customers need a reason to remember you. If you offer loyalty programs, then they will remember you for the offers, services, and visibility you are providing them.

SEO is Worth It

If the COVID-19 scare taught us one thing, it is that connecting with customers online may very well save your company. Business that has been able to survive and thrive during the pandemic were able to do so by flexibly adapting to the purchase experience and by adapting to the needs of the customers. Online visibility was one of the greatest way companies used for protecting their business during the pandemic. Since online sales and marketing shrinks the business world to a few lines of programming code, it is critical to the success of your business to evaluate your online presence for speed and durability.

There are effective ways to improve your visibility within the search marketplace and tools utilizing Search Engine Optimization (SEO). It will serve to move your ranking up the charts and make you more available to your prospective customer base. Investing is this area often pays great dividends.

Be Ready for Everything

Not many prognosticators foresaw the impact that COVID-19 had on the marketplace. In light of the fact, that the pandemic was not even on the radar until December 2019, most of the world suddenly found themselves sitting at home and working online. Unfortunately, this surprise event will match others over your business lifecycle, perhaps lesser then COVID-19, or maybe even greater. But nonetheless there will always be incidents to overcome. There will always be unforeseen circumstances, and no one can change that fact.

You need well developed contingency plans in order to ensure that your business survives in the modern world. You need to develop resources that can be accessed when things get tough. Think living in your parent's basement on a larger scale. These types of events will frequently have a dramatic impact on your front-line workers and your lowest-level employees. These employees can be particularly vulnerable to significant changes in the market and it will be important to have a plan on how to address such an event. The best developed plans will seek to protect the business and its employees in a downturn and make them readily available when things get better. Businesses operating in factories had exponential losses during the COVID-19 crisis. Restaurants, theme parks, and the hospitality business in general suffered devastating losses, forcing many to close permanently. It is crucial for your company to assess potential problems and develop solutions in advance of a catastrophe. Be Ready!

Live to Compete

When you own a business, you automatically compete. Always remember what the market was like before you started your business. You must have felt there was a demand that needed to be filled. Understanding this will also prepare you to be watchful of competitors entering your market with the hope of taking a share from you. Good clients seek out the best business partners. You must continuously strive to rank at the top of your category to ensure that you obtain the customer base; those wanting (maybe yearning) for that great experience they can't find anywhere else.

Keep your business ratings high, and your business will be well perceived in the marketplace. Outshine your competitors by producing high-quality products and your company will thrive.

Prioritize Business Growth

One more thing to keep you on the right track is that maintaining a business is not a passive activity. You are not going expand by focusing on today's success. Don't dream of a new branch, product, or service without a clear understanding of where the current business will take you. You cannot assign the growth of your current business to others as you think about new initiatives. Protect your business product by providing leadership that instills in your team—quality execution is mandatory. Developing plans for business expansion is also key, in order to maintain your momentum. But be prepared to make the necessary corrections along the way if you hope to thrive and grow. Make sure you are focused on growing your business intelligently to ensure that you are strong, and your hard work turns into a profit. Then, you can distribute the proceeds to yourself, your team, and your community.

Something to Remember:

Your compass for growth in your market is designed for you to personally track your success and to distance yourself from your peers and competitors so they cannot catch up with you in any significant way.

Chapter 7

How Many of Us Have Been Thanked Too Much?

"Feeling gratitude and not expressing it is like wrapping a present and not giving it."

- William Arthur Ward[5]

Ask anyone you run into; you will have a hard time finding a person who thinks they have been thanked enough. Humans are not benevolent species that can work with no expectation of recognition.

---

5 https://www.inc.com/jeff-haden/40-inspiring-motivational-quotes-about-gratitude.html#:~:text=40%20Inspiring%20Motivational%20Quotes%20About%20Gratitude%201%20%22Feeling,you%20always%20show%20a%20profit.%22%20More%20items...%20

If you want your workplace to thrive and grow, then you must believe in the power of gratitude. There are many reasons to show gratitude but mostly, having a culture of gratefulness enhances your experience as a person.

Why Gratitude?

How did corporate retreats become such a famous and commonly used tool for bonding in the workplace? Part of the answer may be found in a published research paper from the University of California, Berkeley, that discussed the impact of a good retreat on the attendee[6]. The consultant concluded that spending three days with each other, without any work pressure or need to compete, grew their bond. The gratitude they were willing to absorb and acknowledge in a low-pressured environment turned into appreciation, empathy, and a deeper connection.

Gratitude should be promoted in the workplace because it allows the employees to feel that there is more purpose in their day-to-day work life. We have all seen employees that have a strong distaste for the conventional workplaces. Gratitude is the steppingstone to an array of positive emotions. Real gratitude will solve many issues and clearly prevent others from taking place.

Here are well-established benefits of a grateful workplace concluded through extensive research.

Positive Emotions

Let's presume that you are presenting a game plan to execute in the next six months. You have done your research and are making

[6] https://greatergood.berkeley.edu/article/item/how_gratitude_can_transform_your_workplace

sure that your presentation will dazzle. But sometimes there are other factors that may impact your execution plan, and your boss may counteract some of the points you make. It's not that there is a problem with the overall project and surely your boss does not have any ill intentions. He or she are simply exercising their role in the process. In this scenario you might feel ambushed. Why?

It may be because you are not totally confident in the position you have presented. Or you may not fully understand some level of structure in the workplace that your boss needs to make clear. With an environment of mutual respect and gratitude, where you and your boss have a good camaraderie, you might forward him the PowerPoint presentation beforehand, so together you can discuss the potential issues that may arise. Once you initiate the meeting, you will be more prepared with answers to the possible queries. In the end, it will prove to be a positive learning experience and the meeting a resounding success.

It is the sense of mutual appreciation that made the project work better. You were expected to prove your performance and the issues raised were not about your presentation. These simple solutions will give you a stronger belief in your workplace, in your system, and how your efforts are appreciated.

Reduced Stress

Many physiological conditions are directly caused by stress. High blood pressure, heart issues, anxiety, and many other problems are related to this condition. That is why it is important to ensure you consider your health as you grow in the workplace. Stress can have a significant impact, so you should develop ways to anticipate stressful situations and also ways to navigate through them. The simple fact is that most people will find something else to do if they feel that stress in the workplace is taking a toll on their health. A simple solution to this problem is to promote appreciation at all levels of the leadership team. Gratitude must be anchored at the grass-root level. Your team will feel better about their experiences if they are working in an environment that recognizes how mutual appreciation is critical.

A Sense of Achievement

Feeling good about your workplace is not simply being able to recollect your accomplishments. It is often more important to understand where your accomplishments fit in with the overall corporate strategies. There are often times where it is difficult to see exactly where your work fits in. This factor can lead to some misunderstanding of the role you play in achieving the corporation's success. This is where middle managers and leadership makes the biggest difference. It is critical for managers to provide regular reinforcement for good work and achievement of results. Letting it stand as simply part of the job will not pay long term benefits. Making a difference with positive feedback yields great results for long term success. Many of the younger generation are ambivalent about the workplaces they inhabit. Sometimes the cause of this is that educational systems are heavily designed to recognize students for their performance. This is perfectly aligned with getting good grades for good work, which translates into positive feedback. Most workplaces do not tend to have any reward system designed to recognize intermediate milestones and behaviors. One of the great ways to counteract this need for frequent reinforcement, is simply to demonstrate appreciation for the work being provided. Develop a team of people who recognize each other for achievements and contributions. Simply waiting for the overall goal, will diminish the opportunities to call out great contributions. Take the time to demonstrate the team members achievements on an ongoing basis. Provide an environment that will not simply recognize good performance, during the annual review process. Do it often and mean it!

Remember GSI?

The workplace is a great place for people to learn how life's journey unfolds. Embracing your role in the organization and the role that others play in its overall success, can give you great pleasure as you grow in your position. Understand how an environment can be created that fosters appreciation and support, and people will look forward to work each day.

4 Keys to Gratitude

When it comes to gratitude, our knowledge is surprisingly limited, which is why it makes sense to understand the four key aspects of gratitude that come into play when workplaces embrace it.

Gratitude for Person[7]

We should not be grateful simply for the job a person does, but the person they are, as well. A simple exercise is to place a person in the center of the group and ask everyone to say something nice about them. People will hesitate and shy away at first, but eventually, everyone will end up laughing and encouraging each other. Of course, our boss appreciates when we do a good job, but we also need to feel validated personally. It is important to find ways to have well developed business relationships if we are going to share and

---

[7] https://mike-robbins.com/the-power-of-gratitude/

sustain our gratitude in the workplace.

Customize Your Gesture

One person will love the *thank you* note you gave them. The other person may not. How do you say *thank you* to that person? Do you bring them a cup of coffee and talk to them about their interests for half an hour? Gratitude is not a check-the-box exercise. It is an ongoing process and people should not believe that the person to who you are directing your gratitude must feel the same way.

Leadership-Based Gratitude

Rather than giving a corporate gift with standard tags, try encouraging your leadership team to send thoughtful notes to their team. The gift and the gestures will multiply by manifold if the leaders are involved in the gift exchanges. The benefit of nameless corporate retreats with hundreds of employees is often not an efficient use of time or money. It is often just the personal message of gratitude that resonates a clear message of appreciation to your team.

Gratitude as a Culture

You must ensure that gratitude is a part of the workplace culture if you expect your team mates to reciprocate with others, especially when you are not looking. The workers are deeply incentivized to focus on the underlying cultures that the workplace reinforces. This is why you should make sure that the culture you promote is positive.

We will discuss exercises that will help you develop a stronger workplace culture, but you have to make sure that the culture is based on gratitude. Most of these efforts will become commonplace if the employees feel that the company is pushing them to have an attitude of empathy and appreciation.

Something to Remember:

Embracing your role in the organization and the role that others play in its overall success can give you great pleasure, as you grow in your position.

Chapter 8
Every Manager Teaches Us Something

"A successful man is one who can lay a firm foundation with the bricks others have thrown at him." – David Brinkley[8]

Like a teacher in classroom, both good and bad managers can teach you something about your workplace. Just make sure that you are learning the right lessons, even from the not-so-good bosses.

---

8 https://fitsmallbusiness.com/management-quotes/#:~:text=%2028%20Most%20Inspiring%20Management%20Quotes%20%201,Altes.%20Basically%2C%20it%20means%20that%20success...%20More%20

There are tricks to learning from good experiences, as well as bad encounters in the workplace.

How to Learn from a Bad Boss

Bosses who are not positive or do not encourage you to push yourself further are also destined to teach you a few things.

Is your boss showing too much favoritism in the workplace? You can learn not to show favoritism. Is your boss focused on hoarding the credit? You can learn how to share credit to strengthen the team.

There are many ways to learn from a boss who is ineffective. Observing how these bosses hurt team morale will help you understand how you can boost your team spirit.

Understand Your Purpose

The one positive aspect of having an unappreciative boss is that you get to ask yourself, why are you there? Are you there simply to get praise from a boss? Or are you there to grow your career and clear your path? Are you working in a job where the opinion of one person will decide whether you are good employee or not? If your boss bad-mouths you, those around you will often adopt the same attitude and treat you differently. Professional ramifications notwithstanding, just when a boss openly disowns the employee, the employee goes through an unfair process of treatment.

If your boss is not a very nice person, he/she will most certainly complain against you unfairly. And you will have to answer for the sins you never committed. It does not mean that you will have an excuse for not measuring up, after all, you worked hard to get to that point, so do not let your bad experience ultimately decide your future.

Make sure you are making the best of a bad situation. Learn new skills, make your performance top-notch, and ignore the challenges that are a part of the deal. The less your problems with your boss affect your performance, the better your personal development and performance will be. Be mindful of your experience. Even a bad boss could be the best teacher you have.

Sharpen Your Communication Skills

Has your boss scolded you for a job he assigned to you? It happens all the time in a relationship that is not working. People get scolded more often than reasonable, to the point they feel as though they cannot do anything right. These are tough times and will pass. But you need to be persistent and make sure that you are getting your job responsibilities completed.

Ultimately, a good way to improve communication is simply to deliver results. Did your boss change the deadline? If you have to, stay up all night to complete the assignment. Companies have a hard time criticizing employee who deliver results. Always focus on being an asset at the end of the day, and you will continue to have a personally rewarding experience in the workplace. Eventually the boss will get it!

Conflict Resolution Skills

Conflict resolution isn't new-age ideology, it's generally effective in helping you get through to your bosses and coworkers. You must understand the ways to communicate in all types of environments, be they high pressure or low. The workplace can become a highly pressurized system where the tempers are short, and the hours are long. In these situations, it is exceptionally significant that you learn how to hold your ground without losing your temper or falling apart. These skills can be learned through experience in the workplace. You might consider enrolling yourself in conflict resolution classes, as these may prepare you for what comes your way!

Above are a few major skills you need to understand if you are planning to survive in a challenging environment. You need to learn these skills and catalog them with great introspection. Mastering them will help you become a strong player in your workplace and someone others can turn to. Now for the fun part!

How to Build Your Team

Every supervisor must learn the art of building a team. A person is as good as the team they build. If your team believes that you are an asset, then you are an asset to your organization. It is a fascinating dynamic. In the early part of anyone's career, once the supervisor hires the employees and brings them into the fold, they often train them in areas that are relative to the company culture. But as soon as the employees are established, the success of the supervisor is assessed by the performance of the team. Here are a few effective ways for you to create a strong team for your company.

Have a Face-to-Face Conversation

In today's world, email communication may seem like the best way to communicate, but sometimes it is simply not as effective. Most people dash off an email without carefully thinking it through, as a means of expediency. However, anger emails seem to always find their way back to you. Always make a point to have important conversations face to face, even if it's just a follow-up. Understand that the first conversation may very well be the beginning of a lengthy interaction. Begin the conversation and then give the teammate adequate time to respond. Most importantly, discussions relating to critical executable items should be managed on a personal level, because emails alone may lead to misdirection and potentially serious issues.

Mentors for Everyone

Being new in the company can have its own set of challenges. The system, workplace policies, and many other factors that are sometimes challenging to decipher. Busy supervisors cannot always be there when their employees need guidance. It is a great strategy to assign senior employees as mentors to new employees. They can be available when the employees need help, seek guidance, or simply need to burn off steam.

Make SOPs

If you occupy the role as a leader within any company, people will actually expect some leadership. Part of the challenge is that you will often be torn between getting your job done and making sure others do the same. One method of corralling these challenges is to develop clear standard operating procedures or SOPs. SOPs are the best way to make sure that employees adhere to some or all of the desired activities. This is particularly true within departments where communication challenges exist. If you relocated all of your direct reports into your office for the day, then communication would be easy, but you wouldn't get any work done. SOPs allow for the team to act independently while still understanding where the guardrails are. Establish SOPs for the important aspects of the workplace. From the process of conducting major operations to customer management to human resource policies. The more defined material available for the employees, the fewer issues will arise. Always make a point to work with fellow team members to develop SOPs as they are usually more proficient in their field/department activities needing oversight. Make your SOPs as realistic as possible and make sure that the team understands and embraces their importance.

Stay in Touch

Managers must always remain aware of their surroundings and look for indicators that may assist in managing the team. This is not about intruding on your team to interrupt their workflow, but to be situationally aware of those things that happen around the office. Awareness will assist the manager in being prepared when issues develop and also foster ways to recognize team contributions and successes. Use this awareness to show your team that they are important and that they share in your journey. It is vital that you also understand your ecosystem, as a means of providing leadership for your team. The best way to make sure that you are updated is to understand what senior management is tracking. Your team clearly will expect that you are their interface with the higher-ups. Great leaders will convey to their team, activities and actions that are afoot. This may potentially impact the team in the long run and allows the team to embrace the role they played in the overall success of the company.

Be Realistic

We are all replaceable. When things change, perspectives change as well. As I will describe in more detail in Chapter 11 on Ancient Tribes, supervisors who do not keep up with the changing tides are mostly left behind. This is why you must understand that your contribution is an important component of your organization's success. Understand the goals and be realistic with your team. Being truthful and practical are critical tools to achieving long term success for your team.

Teach Them to Learn

Employees learn from their surroundings. If your employees know that you are a passionate expert in your field and that you are always seeking new and innovative ways to succeed, then they will ultimately learn more, intentionally or otherwise. Make sure your employees see you as a resource , someone they can turn to, in order to develop as significant contributors to the group's success and to the organization long term.

Your employees will often view the workplace from the perspective that you develop. You drive the morale and trajectory of your team. An environment where everyone is pulling on the same rope, utilizing the same resources, will achieve results. Work hard on the quality of engagement, personal accountability, and the value of your work product. Make sure you are delivering the right mindset in the workplace and you will truly have a team that delivers results.

<u>Something to Remember:</u>

Always focus on being an asset at the end of the day, and you will continue to have a personally rewarding experience in the workplace, eventually they will get it!

Chapter 9
Dress for The Job You Want

"Leadership is not about the next election, it's about the next generation." - Simon Sinek

We all look to move up in the workplace. Who does not want the promotion? But have you ever asked yourself how bosses choose the employees they will promote? Employers have a deep and complex relationship with their employees. You need to have the ability to develop strong relationships to survive in the workplace. Similarly, your superior must have a long and mutually supportive working relationship with your team. Without making it a dubious game of "survival of the fittest." how do you develop your workplace skills, to effectively to put you in line to be considered for the next promotion?

The Next Generation

Understand that promotions should have little, if anything, to do with the popularity contests. Although it is often not the case, it is still easy to develop a perception that you are up for a promotion, which might not be shared with your supervisor. As you develop in the workplace you will gain a sense that you may be in consideration for a promotion. When selecting team members for promotion, seldom do employers take a vote among your peers. Your employers are not going to ask for a consensus from the office and probably will not factor in the opinions of your peers. Although, they will take careful consideration regarding your ability to demonstrate leadership skills. Most team members know who is next in line based on their own observations and the skills displayed by teammates. What employers looking for in employees being considered for promotion? They desire the next generation of executives that will ultimately run their company. They need employees who will sit with them at the table and be a part of their world. Here are a few ways you can become the best choice for a promotion.

Dress Well

The more you dress well, the better suited you are for promotion. This is mostly metaphor, insofar as, *Dressing for Success* is a mentality that will support your long-term company goals. This simple statement is more about how you are mentally prepared for greater responsibility rather than the clothes you wear. Dress really means how prepared are you for that special emergency when it arises. Those who respond with a plan and follow through with the execution, are the ones who will surface as the problem solvers.

Some simple-to-fix issues can brutally murder your chances of a promotion. Your boss is flying in from out of state and will not have the time or patience to understand your professional decisions pertaining to a problem. But the boss will clearly be capable of understanding the solutions that you provide. Often, they need to quickly assess your performance, workplace dynamics, expectations, and a few other aspects in one meeting. Leaders who are considering team members for promotion will need to know how you operate under pressure. Being ready for meet the next challenge will take you down the promotion lane far faster than simply doing a great job. So, it is critical that each individual in the workplace be ready for today's challenges and equally prepared for what may come their way. Being physically and mentally *dressed* for success.

Have a Deep Understanding of the Company

With today's information overload, it is impossible NOT to find important information regarding a company on the internet. Even the smallest of companies have websites and Yelp reviews that can give you a simple-to-complex understanding of the organization. Before you go for an interview, look up the company and gather all the information available on them on the internet and study it well. This type of preparation is critical to demonstrating your keen interest in the business and also prepares you for questions relating to the job for which you are applying. Once you have studied as much as you can, then you will be ready to take on the interview. (PS: Taking notes about what you learned will impress the interviewer.) During the interview, give a clear reason for joining the firm. If it is a startup, you can say that you are truly energized by their business model and always wanted to work in an entrepreneurial environment. If it is an established company, you can say that you like established organizations and how they take on their challenges.

The interview it is as much about what you bring to the table, as it is about how you see yourself fitting in. Seek a clear understanding of the direction that the company is taking. In real life, employees who are committed to the company portfolio are preferred over employees who are solely creative thinkers without execution skills or long-term professional goals.

Promotions are the opportunity for the employee to delve deeper into the company and assimilate further into the future of the business. That will only be possible if you demonstrate a commitment to developing as the person who can contribute to the future of the company. The interview will seldom be solely about remembering statistics and more about how your selection will add value to the team and the organization. Simply demonstrate a reasonable understanding of the workplace and how it fits with your skill set and flexibility to grow.

Understand the Workplace

You should not seek to be a referee in every fight of the team. Generally, the situation will sort itself out, but it is good to be the one who can clean up messes when they arise. Most employers tend to respect employees who are less of a problem and more of a solution. If complications and issues are going on in the team, avoid being a part of the gang and be more the provider of strategies to achieve results and change. Rarely do employers like individual employees who team up to control the agenda of the team. If you must be in the gang, make sure you are the leader because it is generally the leaders in the workplace who get things done, who surprise a few people along the way!

Don't take your Foot off the Gas

No matter how complex the workplace becomes, focusing on the target will still yield the best results. Albert Einstein said, *"One way to keep momentum going is to have constantly greater goals."* Most individuals find it very challenging to work in high stress environments. They often find it difficult to face the daily grind. But the fact is, these scenarios are always going to be a part of your work life and will serve as a means of developing the skills needed to achieve success and growth. Rather than quitting the job when the going gets tough, double down and finish it regardless of the time commitment needed. This will surely pay dividends later. Once you focus on the daily strategies for success, your mind will train itself to seek out the challenging work in the workplace. Soon, you will be working in a hurricane of office activity and will focus on progress. Moving forward is the key! Observers will begin to understand just how much can be accomplished when you keep your foot on the gas!

There are almost always two choices in the workplace for individuals to ponder as they effectively tackle the workplace environment. You either quit and move on (mentally or physically) or train your mind to prioritize your work and focus on developing a success attitude. An often-paraphrased quote says, *"you leave because you are either running away from something you dislike, or you are running toward something you enjoy."* Once you develop daily plans and prioritize your work, your mind will be much more inclined to remain focused, no matter how much noise there is in the background.

Upgrade

Invariably, all managers review a wide range of employee characteristics as they consider promoting an employee and they will most often seek those who take on the challenges and look beyond the current goal line. Sometimes, I find it is a little surprising when I meet recent graduates, who only take pride in the idea that they have finished their education. But what they really need to embrace is how much they have to learn! In this day and age, the concept of finishing your education is simply not possible. You will continue to develop, in your skills, capabilities, and expertise, for many years to come. Learning never stops.

I have often heard a coworker say, "I've been in this business for 25 years and have seen everything!" That may be true, but only the last five really matter. Those early years taught him some skills and strategies that came in handy, but what we learn today will truly impact what we accomplish tomorrow. If you apply the fundamental understanding necessary with the day-to-day learning, it will truly prepare you for what's next. There are plenty of examples of engineers who cut their teeth on C++ and Java. What they really need to know is how to utilize the current technology like Python and Angular. The earlier skills may have taught you many things but the most important thing you learned was to keep learning! That is why when you think of software engineers who have been in the field for 20 years, consider the individuals who must learn and upgrade perpetually as a means of staying ahead in the game.

There are plenty more examples in today's workplace. You may have a strong work ethic, a great way to manage your workload, and great office rapport, but you will still face challenges if you do not learn to continuously retool.

Acknowledge the Praise

If your boss praises you, share a *thank-you* note with the team and those you serve. The modern workplace will always have a strong internal communication component and there is no point in taking any part of it for granted. Make sure you document all the praise you have received because there are times ahead where these encouraging messages will come in handy. Bosses deal with uncertainty and lots of developing circumstances, so sometimes, past praises serve as a personal reminder when the going gets tough.

Don't Drop the Ball

All the employees get the proverbial ball now and then. Imagine your employer is out of town and the client calls in the middle of the night with an emergency. You need to be the one who deals with the client, makes them happy, and sends them home with a raving review. Always try to prepare for such events. These are the requirements of the workplace are, even if it is not a part of your daily routine. What software is used? What do the clients need? How to contact customer service? These questions can suddenly show up on your desk and you may need to professionally manage them on your own.

In these circumstances, it is critical to understand that dropping or not dropping the ball is the difference between spending some time in the limelight or not. The simple trick to catching the ball and knocking it out of the park is to know your clients. Most newcomers and younger employees are not assigned to those areas close to the customer until they have developed a level of trust and understanding, therefore they tend to steer clear of the action. They know that if they have done their job, they are good for now. It is not forward thinking to process in that manner. Team members must stay updated on all the client's activities so that if they must step in for a client, they are ready. Stay updated on the latest work being done for the client, not simply by you and those around you, but by the overall work group, it will pay dividends. These simple steps will help you stay prepared for all the actions you can face in the workplace, on short notice.

In conclusion, the promotion has less to do with your official performance and how you work in the office but much more to do with how you will manage the employees and the employer. Your leadership will ultimately keep tabs on the events that occur in the office. While most employees tend to focus on their experience and feel that if it was a positive, then they will succeed, which is often not the case. The reality is that you are continuously supporting the company as it works toward growth.

<u>Something to Remember:</u>

Once you focus on the daily strategies for success, your mind will train itself to seek out the challenging work in the workplace.

Chapter 10

First Remember What Got You Here, Then Think about Where You Are Going

" People who believe they can succeed see opportunities where others see threats." Marshall Goldsmith

The personal journey through the world of work is long. It is easy for a person to get bogged down with the day-to-day battles so much so that they can easily lose sight of the bigger picture. Let's say you have been in your field for ten years and your journey has taken many ups and downs. How do you make sure that you are taking account of your accomplishments and planning carefully? Who is in charge of that?

Sometimes if you stand too close to a brick wall you cannot see the best way to get around it! It can be challenging to understand how your current career path is developing when you feel like a bug on the windshield called work. But those who see the bigger picture, early on in their career, can see the fruits of their labor and develop a deeper perspective. Sometimes you need a GPS, sometimes just a compass to see North and South and sometimes you need to just look out the window to see where you have been and where you are heading! You need to continuously evaluate where your journey is headed if you will have the work-life you deserve.

Here we will outline a few simple ways to *audit* your career path and understand ways for you to grow your career through introspection.

Track Accomplishments

How do you keep track of when you are doing a good job in your workplace? Unless you get a commendation certificate, that is rarely given, most companies do not spend enough time acknowledging successes. Employees must continuously be alert of positive comments and encouraging feedback as a means of visualizing yourself as a growing employee of the company. Learn how to acknowledge and remind your employers and supervisors of the encouragement they gave you a while back and learn how to share the same encouragement with your teammates and those who work for you.

Suppose you gave a good idea to solve a problem in the meeting and got a good response. Make sure you pursue the idea and keep the encouraging supervisor updated on the progress of the idea. Regardless of your beliefs, most supervisors remember when they give an encouraging nod to their employees.

They also have an obligation to make mental notes as to when the employees do not take their encouragement or suggestion seriously. If you do not act on the instructions or follow-up from your supervisor, then you will have missed an opportunity to grow in the workplace and in their perception of you. Generally, I encourage you to make sure you are keeping track of positive remarks and leadership guidance and pursue that encouragement effectively and in a useful way for your personal development and the organization.

Target and Track Your Training

Upskilling is a science, not an art. You need to know how to upscale successfully to grow within your organization and to develop the skills that will help you in this job and the next. Here are a few suggestions concerning upscaling that might help you to focus. For example, it is always best to first upscale in your current niche. There will be time to work on other horizons in the future, but it will pay dividends if you skill up in areas that will be demonstrated in your interaction with the team, today. "Oh wow. Where did you learn that?" questions are what you want to hear.

Most employees these days work within an office setting with multiple disciplines and therefore see many other fields of expertise in action. All of these interactions will provide you with questions you will need to answer and positions you may want to pursue. Be patient, with purpose.

Keep Track of Promotion Attributes

Sometimes there is the perception that the workplace has a culture that the promotions are sometimes not 'fair'. In my personal observations, that's usually not the case. As I mentioned previously, promotions are generally not simply a popularity contest but based on performance, skill and commitment but it also helps to be a team player. Identifying candidates is an ongoing process that all supervisors utilize in both a formal and informal manner that allows them to categorize the attributes and characteristics they see in their team. They will review this "card catalog' of attributes when they are considering a promotion or new position and use them to arrive at their list of candidates. This is often the list that supervisors turn to when an unplanned opening or work project surfaces and resources need to be identified quickly. This is also a way for a leadership team to shortlist the people they want to move up. Every company has an unwritten rule about the set of skills they want to see in their best employee. These skillsets are easy to identify once you pay closer attention to the employees who are promoted.

Ask yourself, what aspects of their personality, work ethic, education, qualification, or experience is shared by all of the promoted employees? Carefully look at the universally identical characteristics and ask yourself, "do I have these characteristics"? The answer will either be yes, in which case, you should polish and strengthen your skillset to give it a stronger presence. But if the answer is no, then you should either work on those skills to improve your chances or find a better-suited company where you can apply your skills. Long term thinking is important and therefore, if you do not expect to be promoted within the company over a reasonable length of time, then you should avoid wasting half a decade in that workplace. Gain a reasonable experience and then switch to a company where you can be recognized for your skills and contribution and ultimately anticipate being promoted.

Learn to Communicate

It is clearly important, now more than ever, to watch what you say. There is plenty of pressure in modern workplaces to say the right thing. It really is important to say the right phrase, in the right way, and at the right time. All of these expectations, when assembled together, might seem like an undue burden on a you but understanding human dynamics will greatly enhance your skills as a team player and a leader. What is the right point to raise in front of your supervisor, or fellow team members, at the right time? Employees must understand how critical it is to demonstrate a clear grasp of communication strategies. You will often communicate differently if you are talking to fellow team members than you will with a client visiting your office from the outside. Understand this variability is also critical when discussing important issues with your boss, and even more importantly with his or her boss. You will reap great dividends if you master the communication methods that allow you to handle unique situations with unique communication strategies. Most important to any communication strategy is knowing when to use which one!

Pitch in

It is generally a significant factor for leadership, when considering teammates for promotion that they consider those times where the employees went above and beyond. If you pitch in to achieve success not for the glory, not for the pay but to get it done, then leadership will remember it. Sometimes these situations present themselves and you must think quickly and act accordingly to do what it takes to get it done. If the roof starts leaking, start looking for buckets, if the bus stops running, grab a gas can and if the project gets stalled then find those who can get it back on track. There is almost always room at the table when you want to make a difference. One of the pre-requisites for getting to the table is to commit to doing your work impeccably. If you are always doing your job well and can kick in where needed to assist other departments in achieving their goals, the team is ready for you to be at the table. Another point to remember is that if you are given a new task and, you can't create the solution from your knowledge alone, no matter how extensive, then you know exactly who to turn to. Eventually, people will start keeping you updated, even when you aren't on the team to seek your input and recommendations, so stay connected!

One-Person Show, not

Organizationally, one person shows don't really stand out in the hall of fame of projects that change the company. They are often '*got to have*' activities but short lived. Make your plans simple and avoid including too many of your colleagues in the execution plan and keep it short. Because time is always of the essence and the small projects need rapid execution, you should ask around when you are creating a plan if you need others to be included. But make sure you test the interested colleagues before adding them to the final project. Gotta get it done!

Learn to Assess

One of the greatest tools that you can use to chart your workplace journey is to look back on what you have accomplished and remember what it took for you to get there. Assessing those activities, that paid the highest dividends, will be those you utilize in the future when you face similar situations. It will also give you a clear understanding of what you should NOT do. Generally, small failures won't crater a project but will force leadership to assess and adjust. Take the lesson learned that took you down the wrong backstreet and remember them next time you are at the crossroads. This type of activity stacking will help you make progress much more quickly as you develop, you ultimately will not make the same mistakes. You will also focus on those items that made the biggest difference. These lessons should not be wasted solely on you, as you should always take the time to lead your team in understanding the merits of assessment and strategizing for next time.

It is also important to adopt your employer's perspective as in every action you take toward a shared goal will be the opportunity to help them see you as the asset you have become. Keep a close eye on how your employers address you and read their comments carefully. You will need to understand their perspective as a compulsory part of your career growth plan.

A simple way to understand their perspective is to network in your niche industry. Having a network strengthens your standing in the workplace because you have resources and contacts in the industry. More importantly, it will allow you to have interaction with others who face similar situations and give you something to use when you need it. Most individuals will occasionally find themselves in seemingly impossible scenarios You will need to see the world from all perspectives so that you can combine your own perceptions with your mentor who can elaborate on those alien mindsets that you might not see. Always be looking forward and carrying those skills you have learned in your '*backpa*ck'.

Something to Remember:

It can be challenging to understand how your current career path is developing when you feel like a bug on the windshield

called work. But those who see the bigger picture, early on in their career, can see the fruits of their labor and develop a deeper perspective.

Chapter 11
Members of the Ancient Tribes Who Did Not Get Along, Got Eaten!

" The reason life works at all is that not everyone in your tribe is nuts on the same day." Anne Lamont

Generally, the 'odd one out' happens for a reason. There are plenty of employment laws concerning terminating employees. Admittedly, they are present for a good reason. Still, as you seek to operate your company, group, or team, you have to ensure that your employees are part of the solution and not the problem[9]. If you think of it this

---

9   https://www.forbes.com/sites/mikekappel/2017/04/05/5-

way, it may help. You are operating a machine and every part of the machine costs you money, hopefully it generates a return. You cannot afford to have a piece of machinery that is not synced with the overall team. Your machine needs to operate in sync if you want it to work well. It can seriously undermine your productivity, and outcomes, if the entire machine is not focused on the intermediate and long-term goals.

There are many developing situations where an employer determines that the prospective employee will be a great fit for the organization and contribute greatly to its success. Often times employers hire an employee with high hopes, but over the near term do not measure up to the expectations they sensed just a few months prior. The result is that they have a critical employee who is not a part of the effective solution matrix. What now? They have to let them go in a manner which allows them some comfort and ultimately leads to a positive experience. How will you do that? Here are a few ways to make sure that you are transitioning employees in an effective and appropriate way.

Clarity Is Important

There are times when it will be necessary to provide negative feedback or terminating employment of a teammate. You will find that the employee, once they discover the reason for the meeting will listen less and generally distress more. Therefore, it is critical for you to be prepared with clear facts that illustrate the difference between the last time you reviewed their performance and today, as you prepare for termination. Be direct and do not beat around the bush. Make sure you clearly illustrate what brought them to this
tips-on-how-to-fire-an-employee-gracefully/?sh=68cbb8a329dd

point in their employment. I have often said to managers that if the reasons that an employee is being terminated is a surprise for them, then you have not communicated well. There should be no surprise when the final moment comes. Even though the moment may be tense, it is important that you speak professionally and deliberately. Employees may not hear the message, as they are processing your comments, so it is critical to be direct and you must keep your own emotions under control if you are to communicate with impact. Remembering that the purpose of your meeting, It is either to improve performance and you are engaging the employee in a self-assessment, or it is a termination, and you should be brief and direct.

It is often advisable to gain a common understanding that the topics of conversation are not unique and that the items under consideration have been covered in the past in personal and professional meetings. State simply the reason for the meeting and you may even have a few encouraging points. That way, the employee will know that you have evaluated their overall performance and that characteristics that were demonstrated were accurate. Your positive remarks will not contest the termination if you clearly define the negative points that make the termination a necessity and the negative points are valid and well justified[10]. If the employee does not have a clear understanding of his or her shortcomings, then you, as the leader, have not communicated clearly in the past. If it's a surprise, you haven't done your job. Again, the termination should never be a surprise to the employee

Outline Your Expectations in the Interview

As we related to ancient tribes and the teamwork necessary to be safe
10   https://www.inc.com/suzanne-lucas/10-simple-ways-to-get-an-employee-to-quit.html

and secure in their world, each team member has an important role in the tribe and must seek to accomplish those goals so that others can focus on their objectives. If you are in charge of watching the cave to prevent wild animals from entering and you do not accomplish your assignment, then those preparing the meal might not be successful either. They might even get eaten in the process. So, it is critical for team members to realize the role they play individually as well as their part in the overall plan. In the efficient workplace, every employee is told about their role in the organization, but leaders must also effectively lay out the individual job requirements. You need to make sure you have outlined the basic expectations that you have for the employee. Otherwise, you will have to look inwardly if they do not achieve the goals and you have yourself to blame for the misunderstanding. It is also important to have a strong job description when the position is advertised and or offered. Job descriptions should include all aspect of the job requirement, including social expectations, if there are any. If the job ultimately has more requirements than were discussed in the hiring interview, then it again is the fault of the leader.

Reasons for Changing Teammates

As we said earlier, firing an employee is not generally about proving that they are incompetent. It is about showing that the desired results and actions, after careful review, were not delivered. As the title of this chapter indicates, the overall leadership of the project is in the hands of the manager and those who cannot contribute must be identified. Careful planning is necessary for a manager to illustrate why teammates assigned to a project are not a good fit. One-on-one evaluations, as well as team leadership discussions, provide the necessary support for a decision. If you have a project that needs to be delivered in four months and one of the employees regularly faces delivery challenges holding back the team, then it is critical to make the necessary decision to eliminate the unproductive team member. This could simply be a situation of a poor fit, and a reassignment to another project, team, or department may serve the organization better. The critical role of the supervisor is to make a timely decision. The longer you wait, the more challenged the environment for the other team members will become.

Keep the Team Informed

As a project has the wheels coming off, and the team is working overtime to get it done, it is critical that they realize that you, as manager, are taking measures to correct the situation. You identify where the challenges are in the project and they will close ranks to get it done. Those managers who are most successful managing teams are the ones who communicate well to the challenged employee, so much so that the employee often times will come to the leader and request a change. This bodes well for the team as well, as they will have often developed a relationship with the challenged employee and have personal feelings about their departure. This will cause them to look for a fair resolution. Alternatively, if the situation becomes a confrontational environment, it can easily affect all team members. Employees can become disheartened and lose focus. A clean separation is in the best interest of all parties involved. It will also be clear to your fellow teammates about the methods you employ when dealing with performance issues. That fairness and respect will go a long way for the remaining team members to understand how they can expect to be treated.

One important factor that managers must consider, was discussed in

Chapter 2, titled, Right Sizing is Right When you are Left, is survivor syndrome. Those who are left after the departure of the employee are often faced with an increase in duties and responsibilities. More often than not, the team is more than happy to close ranks rather than tolerate an underperforming teammate.

Don't do It Alone

In these litigious times, it is critical to utilize the human resources (HR) of your company in developing an orderly transition for problem employees. This may be common knowledge, but this practice cannot be overstated. Once the decision has been made and you have discussed the outcome with your managers, then having a witness present is a good practice. Employees react in various ways when they are demoted or fired. Support for the interaction and final meeting is critical. One of the great challenges in today's workplace is the link between social media and the workplace. LinkedIn, Facebook, and other platforms provide employees with interaction with associates and similarly positioned people at other companies. Employment changes and actions can often times lead to increased "chatter" on social media platforms that may negatively cast light on your organization. You might find the entire interaction summarized on LinkedIn. Now your PR manager gets involved and provides you feedback on handling crisis during challenging times.

If you have made the decision to terminate the employee, then clearly outline the recent issues in their lack of performance and discuss how these are important to the project. Finally, tell them in clear terms that they have been terminated and you wish them the best of luck. You must stay close to these outlined pointers and you will have a good experience.

Announce to the Team

Do not remove an employee from your team without planning for the follow-up meeting with those who remain. The message must come directly from you. You will want to demonstrate to the team that they have your continued support through the subsequent transition. Have a meeting with your employees that clearly delineates the transition plan and how each of them is even more critical to the success of the project. By doing this, the other employees will know that they have not been blindsided by the anticipated change and will willingly step up. They will know they are in the loop and they can be there for their teammates if they want to help.

Letting your employees go is a part of your business management skill. Most of the time, it will not be a single issue that results in a change or termination. It is important to have a clear protocol that allows you to do your job clearly and do it well. Uncertainty will be a serious problem, so make sure you are making a plan that your team can follow successfully.

Check up with other employees and take their temperature when you are transitioning employees. A terminated long-term employee may have close ties and loyalty they may use in a way that might not be supportive. So, you must over communicate.

Something to Remember:

It is critical for team members to realize the role they play individually, as well as their part in the overall plan.

Chapter 12
Helping Others Help You

" When we give cheerfully and accept gratefully, everyone is blessed." Maya Angelou

Kindness can be contagious. It can be the basis for a positive workplace experience. A place where you will spend most of your days for the foreseeable future. As a result, it will be the factor that drives your emotional outlook and frequently carry over to your personal life. You might ask yourself, "How do I breed this positive environment in order to have an optimal workplace experience? Start with understanding the true nature of kindness and caring in the workplace. Here, is a list of a few significant kindness experiences that many of us will encounter in our lifetimes. When seen from a new perspective, these experiences may assist you in viewing your team in a new light and add greater value to working together.

Politeness is Worth It

Holding the door, saying sorry, and saying please may sometimes feel like insignificant gestures. There are even some people who see these as weak behavior patterns. But these are simple ways to show humility and kindness to all. If you are open to simple manners and courtesy, your primary persona will also improve. Courteous behavior in regular workplace interactions is a simple and effective way to create rapport and build trust with your peers. Once your peers see how positive your general energy is, it will translate into greater energy on their part and they naturally become open to a positive environment over which they have control.

Credit Should Go Where the Credit Is Due

It is listed in the acts of kindness but here is another simple rule of the workplace. If you do not deserve credit for any event, then you will not be the only person who knows that the credit does not belong to you. To take a distinction that does not belong and give a victory lap in these situations creates challenges for the team.

Of course it is great to take credit when the outcome was controlled by you, but unless you are incredibly well-liked or well-protected, both your superiors and your underlings are going to find moments where your claim of credit is not deserved and distasteful. Most importantly, it will bring into question your ability to deliver genuine success and give effective results when you need it most. Rather than ignoring others' successes or making excuses, stand beside the successful person and provide positive reinforcement.

Be Nice to the New Person

The new person is well...new. He or she is possibly nervous and does not know much about the workplace. Breaking the ice early with new employees will provide outreach which may last the duration of your tenure with the organization. By introducing yourself on the first day and providing support you will increase the speed with which the new team member reaches to team's goals. Clearly, it helps them to understand who is on the team and who can be approached and trusted early on.

Maybe that person will become the most important member of the team in the coming years. But in any case, positive outreach is an excellent way to start a new experience. First impressions stay with people for a long time. When they look back on their journey through the company, they will remember their early days. So, make sure you develop positive interaction for them to remember and cherish.

Do Small Favors

Most people have a misguided notion that small favors in the workplace are unnecessary, thinking there is simply too much to do! Remember, the provisions you make for small supportive actions for new employees, will generate a greater and more cohesive team in the long run. It may accelerate the learning curve and make your team even more productive. You give them your pencil one day, and they will ask you for your pen the next day. Even though these fears are occasionally valid, the fact is, you can also gain a friend who will be ready to give you the pen next time. It is a risk worth taking when you are better off making emotional investments in your workplace.

There are many different ways these kinds of favors can get out of control, but the general sense of teamwork and comradery are excellent ways to develop a strong bond in your workplace.

We are All Human!

It is easy to assume that we are all fallible and therefore, will make mistakes in life and in work. Team members can take two directions when a colleague makes a major screw-up. They can lose their temper, go into an unreasonable rage, and ultimately regret what comes out of their mouth. Or an even better strategy, is to take a deep breath, politely go out for a walk (either physically or mentally) and come back ready to help the team solve the problem.

The workplace will always have situations that do not go in the direction that the team intended. One of the great actions that supports a person's ability to face challenges is to understand how one can rely on the team. Often times you will have to preemptively condition your mind to approach things in a certain way which equips you to be prepared when a situation arises. Train yourself to review the potential scenarios that may exist regarding your project and you will be able to anticipate the next crisis calmly and challenge yourself not to overreact. These will soon be your conditioned responses, and you will react better and be more successful in these future situations.

Pay it Forward

You are standing at the lunch counter, and the guy behind you has a two-dollar juice box for lunch. Be the nice guy and pay for guy's drink. These small gestures are a great way to develop strong connections in the workplace and an environment for caring.

Many of us have a small group of team members with whom we interact on a daily basis. If you make inroads with other employees in different verticals structures within your organization, you will have the potential for greater access to other departments and develop small but significant connections with unrelated teams. I often employ a very simple method of paying it forward by never taking the change from the vending machine after I have made a purchase. I imagine the surprise when the next person gets more change that they anticipated and have that "I'm kind of lucky" look on their face.

Help others help themselves

When your workplace HR team posts an opening, think of individuals in your network who could benefit. These simple sharing exercises make you a networker and allow your connections to see you as an asset and a team player.

You will probably gain a few good connections at the workplace if one of your network members fills the position. But most significantly, it is an excellent way to show that you are connected with your workplace's needs.

"Small Talk" is OK

It is eight in the morning, and your coffee line is pretty long. You can spend those twenty minutes scrolling through the newsfeed on your cell phone, or you can engage in some casual conversation in the line. Seizing small opportunities to create enthusiasm and project the personal perspective that life is good, will probably wake you up and help you and others feel better about the day.

The day has a chance of ending better if you start your day with an open mind. You will make a few new acquaintances and maybe get a coffee buddy from those brief interactions.

Believe in Causes

Embedded in the mindset of today's populous is the idea that making BIG changes are critical. Elections, stock market or community events tend to attract the modern Millennials and reinforce that change had to come on a significant scale. They may not consider the food drives, clothing drives, petition-signing campaigns, and small advocacy gestures. Change will come from all directions and it is important to channel your energies in areas where you have passion. Making the animal shelter successful can pay great dividends in the community and can "scratch that community itch" that you feel. It also makes you feel good. If you can affect change on a global scale, then go for it, but doing good locally can pay great personal dividends.

Understand that it is also high-quality bonding over a shared passion in the workplace. As most of the general entertainment experiences are considered indulgent, these causes increase workplace congeniality while keeping life simple. These drives and plans should be allowed to help grow the companionship in your workplace.

Nominate Others

As the leader in your work group, you must remember the importance of confidentiality. Make certain that you share the appropriate information with your team members, especially during reviews, so that they can focus on the prior performance and the goals ahead. It is also important to share with your bosses the performance of your colleagues. They will also want to understand which are the quality members and seek to recognize them, as well.

Employers see these reviews as good ways to gauge their future prospects and quality of their leadership. Ensure that you are presenting yourself as a communicative and understanding employee who can be trusted for future evaluations. Being overly negative will not help you grow in your career.

Make Eye Contact Often

One of the easiest, and often ignored, methods of connecting with people is a smile and a warm greeting. Making others feel that their presence is recognized and that they are a part of the team will generate long-term positivity to the environment. A simple greeting at the beginning of the day, can reinforce the team spirit and demonstrate inclusion in the team's efforts. Make sure that your gestures and body language are inviting and not hostile or closed off. In other words, be genuine and mean it! These small gestures are essential factors in your workplace and will facilitate the ability for others to approach you, with both opportunities and concerns.

This again is not about give up personal space by creating a welcoming environment. It is less about how you dress and more about how you carry yourself. These simple approaches will help you grow your network and you will come off as an enthusiastic teammate.

Gift a Book

Many of us keep buying new books all the time. You are holding one right now, thanks! But more importantly, is the fact that giving a book, as a gift, is a great way to connect with a person. It is even more personal if you share a recently completed book with a coworker and speak to some of the great findings you discovered. Rather than sending your extra books to the library for donation, choose a few that you will gift. This simple gesture will help you gain some exposure and engagement with teammates and friends and may allow you to develop deep and lifelong friendships.

In conclusion, workplace networking is an art and not a science. It is not about the endless self-help books and soft skills classes. It is about an everyday interaction and understanding that people will mirror your behavior. If you are open-minded, connective, and ready to mingle, you will soon find like-minded people.

Always understand that you have ambitions to fulfill and goals to reach. These goals will firstly require an open mind and a willing heart. Make sure that you are using an open mind when you are making daily connections. These simple mindset tricks will help you becomes more robust and grow more clearheaded as time passes.

Allow yourself to have a better experience by allowing your surroundings to engage with you. Most workers become overly concerned with occasional gaffs, which can lead to even more significant issues. Try to understand that there is no such thing as a perfect experience at the workplace, but hard work and commitment by you and your team will pay great dividends.

Something to Remember:

Remember that the provisions that you make for small supportive actions for new employees will generate a greater and more cohesive team, in the long run.

Chapter 13

The Environment Drives Success:

It Is up to You

"Surprises always wait for those with the energy and curiosity to look; so always look. Stay surprised and live forever." Garry Fitchett

There are countless organizations that espouse strategies that are designed to drive success. Once such organization is General Motors (GM). General Motors is a celebrated manufacturer in the automotive landscape in the United States and has served a leading role in the development of the automotive industry around the world. The company is unique in its durability within and industry where many automotive giants could not withstand the competitive landscape and have been acquired of forced to shut down. The industrious business model of GM produced its survival strategy, and the company thrived in the continuously changing landscape of the modern automotive industry. This is a great model to dissect as to illustrate how HR can be the driving force for corporate development and as a driver to success. The model was also chosen because of GM's personnel training model which is based on extensive testing and individualized personnel evaluation.

Training and Development

Training and development programs should be utilizing many perceived employee factors, which include principally the aptitude of the employee. Gary Dessler states in his book, *Human Resource Management* that the employee evaluation and testing at the right intervals is an effective means of evaluating the employee's professional aptitude. The reliability and validity of the tests are key to ensuring that the employee is being evaluated on the correct grounds, and of course, with the appropriate frequency. GM employs a long-range of mock tests and assessments that are designed to ensure that not only their employees, but their consultants are also hired based on the right aptitude.

What about the little guys?

Managerial assistance is the key to successful HR policy. So, what can the little guy do to develop strength in communication and programs that support successful teams? Managerial mentorship invites strength in communication from the employees, and the employees tend to respect their chain of command no matter the *length of the chain of command.* At every level, in large organizations and small, there are many ways in which managers can mentor the employees; a few are listed as follows:

One-on-One Mentorship: Online studies, utilizing an algorithm, shows that one-on-one mentorship is by far the best way to ensure high performance from employees. Employees feel more engaged and understood when leaders engage with them, individually, on a frequent basis.

Managerial Evaluation: Feedback and evaluations are often synonymous in small organizations where a formal process is not developed, and casual interaction is king. At larger organizations as well, the process of evaluating team members regularly has shown great promise for personal and organizational growth. 360-degree evaluations have taken internal chat to new level when managers embrace the feedback they receive, either anonymous or identified. In any organization, employees should be allowed to evaluate their managers regularly so that they can assess their leadership and their interaction, giving leaders the opportunity to address issues that arise. Evaluations within all organizations should endeavor to provide team-mates and leadership with an understanding of the climate in which they work and the opportunities which they collectively face.

Timing

Do not wait for disaster to strike before you recognize and/or reward stellar performance. Leaders should always be-on-the-lookout for talent within their teams that can grow within the current environment, as well as into the future. Often the promotion of employees occurs only when other team members are dismissed. This should not be the case. Developmental and promotional opportunities should be available, which are not detrimental to other members positions, but allow for employees to grow at a faster pace within the team. Planning with this in mind provides leadership with a clear plan for the future leaders. It also allows recognition of demonstrated talent, which becomes obvious to the other members of the team. Work hard and be like them!

Mentorship in Organization

Upon a closer look, one will notice that all of these recommendations are heavily based on mentorship from leaders to learners. Reddy & Lakshmi-Keerthi published a paper in 2017, that describes the changing culture of HR analysis. Since Google Inc.'s interest in HR analytics grew, they developed software and analytical tools designed to ensure that HR policies are generated based on data and not human perception of the workplace.

The data has shown that in the cases where one-on-one mentorships are available to the employees, employees tend to like their workplace more. Huh? Amazing. An infamous discussion in the HR world revolves around the fact that most employees do not leave their workplace based on any external factors, other than their immediate supervisors.

These researchers indicate that mentorship is the key to successful organizational HR policy and reduces general stress in the workplace. That is why GM is focused more on mentorship programs, which increases communication among employees.

Employee Orientation and Socialization

Employee recruitment and socialization are two key factors in the employee retention processes. Klein & Weaver conducted a study on the significance of office orientation in 2000, that concluded employees who attend orientation, tend to increase their social circle in the next year. Six criteria of employee socialization were monitored for two months during the orientation training program.

The Study

The study was conducted for 112 employees who were asked to join in a voluntary employee-orientation training session that was aimed to increase organization socialization. The employees did not belong to the same occupation but instead came from diverse professional backgrounds. Employees who attended the orientation improved in three of the six socialization dimensions, (i.e., values, people, and history), while the employees who did not attend the training lagged in those dimensions. The employees who participated in the training also increased organizational commitment. This was an unexpected outcome as the training was not intended to yield this result, but a great surprise.

Replacement Orientation

Often, when an individual is leaving their post, a new employee is oriented into that position. The individual will first mentor the person taking their place and will show him or her their perspective towards goal orientation and problem-solving—the general 'landscape' of working in the department. Because of this transition and because of different background and training, the new individual may attack the same issue with a different perspective and may choose to develop new strategies to solve the issues. Below are some of the steps one might take to orient a replacement employee.

Trouble Shooting: Allow the new person to engage in various organizational issues that you encounter regularly and allow him or her to develop their perspective on how to deal with the problem. This will let them to see the situation from a new perspective and come up with solutions that would have been new to you. This will also yield a great discussion regarding WHY?

Goal Orientation: Show them the realistic goals that you tend to develop, based on the workflow, and ask them to aim to achieve similar results. The process of trying to achieve these goals will let them see the hurdles that commonly arise. Once they have addressed these issues, they will be mentored on how these situations can be dealt with and what are the typical options.

In main aim of the orientation program, was to ensure that they develop their roles, perspectives, and strategies to handle the issues that arise every day. Employees can deal with problems better if they develop their perspectives on how to troubleshoot the issues. If you guide them with an overly intensive approach, they will fail to develop their own personal perspective. They ultimately may be challenged if they have to face these issues alone and may find it more difficult (and take longer) to solve them, ultimately.

The Klein & Weaver report aimed to attach some significance, within an organization, for compassion in the growth of the company and transition leadership. These techniques are designed to exhibit how challenging expectations from new employees can sometimes lead to disappointments that can be avoided. If the managers in a system consider mentorship for their employees regularly, as a personal responsibility, then they can run successful and impressive teams without any issues that will transition well.

Something to Remember:

Planning with this in mind (promotions) provides leadership with a clear plan for the future leaders and also allows recognition of demonstrated talent which becomes obvious to the other members of the team.

Chapter 14
Trust and Be Trusted!

"If you don't know where you are going, you'll end up someplace else." Yogi Berra

Your environment will drive your success factor. If you do not believe me, look at Silicon Valley. Silicon Valley had to employ hundreds of college dropouts, who mostly happened to be introverts. Because of the unconventional upbringing, many times these leaders had no way to understand how to help their employees feel better in a conventional workspace.

Do you know what they did? They threw out the conventional workspace! The world is continuously changing, and you should try to evolve with it. The fact is— do not worry about the contention, as the convention is a moving target.

Employees come first

Well, the employee cannot always be right when your company has a thousand employees, correct? Wrong, when you are managing more employees than you can count, that is exactly when you should have ground rules, with the leadership team, for individual employee management. You must ensure that there is a clear understanding that a strong HR policy in your workplace.

If you are working with ten employees or less, it is normal to go through every employee on a case by case basis. But if you are working with thousands of employees, you need a system that is simple, with basic protocols are set in stone.

Big organizations either develop a courageous and deliberate HR policy that empowers their employees, or they have the potential to shrink drastically because they did not respect their talents. They need to make sure that the workplace has a strong policy to protect their best assets; otherwise, their assets will falter and find something else to do!

Visualize your Vision

Visualization for the sake of employee motivation is a key asset. I have mentioned this earlier as well, but when your employees feel enthusiastic about their jobs, they will be excited about doing them. Let them see how amazing it will be once they achieve the goals they strive for, and soon they will be as interested in achieving your company's vision as you are.

How do you achieve this simple, yet tough goal? By showing your company's achievements in an interesting and compelling manner.

Ge them charged up! When you engage with the productivity profile of your company and make sure that your employees see how they are contributing to the company's growth, they will be compelled to enthusiastically engage with your company's mission and brand.

Work-Life Balance

Work-life balance is the future of your employees. Even if you do have an eye roll every time someone mentions work-life balance, there is compelling evidence that organizational needs will ask for diverse and unique work execution processes.

Let's take COVID-19, for example. The entire world had to move to remote work because of the pandemic. Most employees and bosses were not ready to work from home. But the companies adapted. Many employees began to wonder why they could not work from home, when it was more convenient for them.

Parental leaves, paternity leaves, and yearly vacations are all good reasons for employers to allow flexible and diverse work modes. These modes will help the employees feel at ease and will let them feel that they have a strong balance between work and personal life. This balance will also lead them to have a stronger sense of fairness towards their workplace as they will not feel that they are sacrificing everything for their work.

Good Manager Employee Relationship

We have all heard the statistics that say most employees do not leave the workplace; instead, they leave their bosses. The employee's experience will be defined by the boss. Incentivize your managers, if you want them to promote their underlings.

Managers will work towards the goals they are incentivized to achieve. Most managers are incentivized to have excellent productivity, but they are often not incentivized simply to promote their underlings. There are ways to incentivize succession planning and, not surprisingly; if they are incentivized to promote their underlings then the inter-company promotions will rise at an astonishing level.

One of the common reasons for managers to avoid promoting their underlings, is the fact that the underlings may ultimately take their place. If the workplace hierarchy is adapted to provide horizontal growth and opportunity ceases to be a pyramid in its skeleton, managers will be happy to promote their employees to serve the overall good of the organization.

Teamwork

When we think of teamwork, we all think of those sad "trust exercises" and how much we hated to participate in them. But trust is important to team building, so let's switch the game. Rather than focusing on simple exercises, encourage your employees to praise each other openly.

Create a day where your employees can list the good points their peers shared in the office. Or have a secret admirer day where all of the employees are allowed to drop secret appreciation messages to their peers for all the things that they admire about them.

These simple exercises will help the workplace become friendly and conducive to change. The employees will have greater camaraderie and will have a conduit to express actual satisfaction. That will allow them to have a bigger and deeper understanding of the workplace.

Most employees wonder where they stand in the scheme of things, and having a clear understanding helps them be more productive.

Go Tech!

Technology is the new challenge in everyday workplace scenarios. When it comes to technology, the workplace seems to be in a continuous eye roll. The reason is technology has grown into an endlessly moving target. The world seems to focus on the easier solutions in the industry, and productivity enhancement is the forte of their interests.

This endless obsession is a double-edged sword, in its own right. While the world seems to focus on change, the workplace feels the brunt of endlessly new technology. There were emails, and then IM's, Zoom calls, and now video conferences—all within the last fifteen years.

Even though the change seems relentless at best, and useless at worst, running away from technology, while billions of dollars are being poured into industrial advancements through technology, is certainly not the best course of action. Embrace it.

On-board Better

Onboarding, short for organizational socialization, touched on before, is the reason many employees become dishearten before even beginning their journey with your company. Their credentials are not created properly; no one truly explained to them what their job should be. Have a simple hierarchical chart that outlines the issues and solutions in the regular onboarding process.

If you are working with an experienced employee, then allow them to understand the workplace at their own pace. Ask them to fill out an onboarding form and make sure that you design a program that caters to their needs closely. These are simple but effective steps to help you gain a true perspective of your employees.

Easy Access to Information

Employees get lost in lack of information. They are a part of the project, but they do not have access to all the information, necessary to make the project successful. Based on endless hierarchies, the data is not shared personally by the project manager. Now, it is incumbent on the newcomer to gain the trust of the project manager, in order to gain complete access.

Even if the newly, onboarded employee successfully accomplished the task, but relied on people-pleasing skills, and was not centered on the company or worked to improve its productivity, the employee impedes his or her own productivity. In essence, when employees focus more on making their supervisors happy and less on helping the company grows to its full potential, they do not grow to their full potential.

Now imagine changing one simple step. The employees have access to all the information, and they are able to provide independent ideas and feedback on the portal. This simple step will allow the user to feel more empowered, and whenever they feel that their voice will be better heard, they will willingly use the portal to speak their mind. Here is where technology exhibits real-time value.

These changes in the delivery of power will allow you to have a more pleasant experience and will be illustrated by your company's morale. Have a strong, but simple distribution of power in your workplace and it will lead to a stronger work ethic among your staff.

Most executives are fearful of taking power away from their managers. Primarily, because when they were managers themselves, they saw their authority as a significant factor in company stability.

However, this unreasonable focus on managerial authority, in the modern workplace, has become an issue that is completely blown out of proportion. The more power managers have, the less you will receive from your deserving employees. You will find that the best ideas and their execution are void of powerful solutions. You must hone into your entire workforce and to utilize their full potential.

Employee Coaching Sessions

An employee coaching session is an effective way to help grow your employees. Create a mentorship program where suitable senior employees are invited to coach and mentor the newcomers in the workplace. Incentivize your employees to grow and promote these newcomers through pilot training programs.

Once a staff member has garnered their experience, they should be financially motivated to devise the pilot programs. That will allow the established employees to find gainful experience in helping their peers. These steps will also help to grow and boost the general morale of the company.

The fact is, a healthy workplace, is a productive workplace. If the employers take the opposite approach and create a divisive, competitive environment, it will foster a lack of understanding among its peers. These elements are frequently incentivized when two employees are pitted against each other.

In these moments, I ponder one simple question; if two employees are vying for the same position, why are they expected to compete with each other? This question should be addressed in the workplace if the company expects to have a decent experience with their employees and they compete for the company's success not their own.

Most of the millennial generation has nearly zero tolerance for negative experiences in the workplace. If the workplace turns out to have toxicity, this youthful bunch will just look for a job that gives them a better experience. These are the facts that the modern workplace faces, and why it is prudent to accommodate quality in social cultures.

If your best employees do not feel affection for your workplace. or do not feel that your workplace is an effective place for them, you will lose good talent. This is why good working relationships in the office are crucial.

Something to Remember:

When you engage with the productivity profile of your company and make sure that your employees see how they are contributing to the company's growth, they will be compelled to enthusiastically engage with your company's mission and brand.

Chapter 15

I Learn More When I Listen Then When I Talk

"Most people do not listen with the intent to understand; they listen with the intent to reply." Stephen Covey

The workplace is populated with people of all stripes. Many who like to take control, many who like to be controlled, and many who simply want to be paid every couple of weeks. This chapter speaks to the innate need to understand compatibility within your team and how to maximize it for the overall good. It will also touch on the choices we make when we embark on a career or business. Each comes with its own challenges and rewards.

Deep compatibility is a crucial part of workplace success. We all need a place where synchronicity and understanding among peers flourish, and oftentimes, develop unbreakable bonds. But cultivating trust in your workplace is a tough task, as there are times when the culture in the corporate environment are not conducive to understanding and collective work. The managers role is to determine where the challenges lay and fix them. Understanding this phenomenon requires extraordinary listening skills. The manager needs to decipher from the workplace conversations, if the team is truly focused and what is their strategy to achieve success.

One of the best ways for managers to build trust amongst their employees is to cultivate healthy conversations with the team on a regular basis. It will provide an opportunity to sort through those conversations in order to determine the activities and events that will matter to the ultimate outcome. This task is hard and requires diligence and commitment. Trust among your employees will build your organization. These are a few tips to help you achieve positive results.

Understand Hard Work

It is important to remember that trust is not given but earned. There are going to be many times in the journey, when employee asks himself if he can trust the company. If you are there for your employees in the tough moments, your employees will be there for you in the company's tough times as well. Put responsibility in the hands of those who have earned it. Trust is a byproduct in the search for teammates who are focused on achieving results and demonstrating team leadership. This relies on the ability of the manager to listen and understand what the team is doing and thinking, in order to focus on cultivating overall success. Listen to the team.

Make certain that the hard work you put into building trust is taken as an example to be followed by other members of the team. That will only occur when employees are incentivized to work together and will feel that it will adequately move them towards the overall goals, both personal and professional. Employees will also learn more when they listen to their teammates.

Within the scope of this chapter it is also important to understand the choices that we all make when embarking on a lifelong work experience. Leaders and learners will come to understand what it takes to be successful within the context of the choices that they make. Work can often be dissected into two categories: work for yourself as an entrepreneur or work for others within a company. These are some considerations whether you choose employment or entrepreneurship. In either case, when a leader understands the various choices and develops ways to compensate their employees, they can experience expansion of their work experience and develop greater horizons.

Fixed Vs. Flexible Timetable: Fixed timetable that comes with a job gives you the routine and discipline that is good for developing a personal life. The flexible timetable of business makes you creative and encourages you to push your boundaries. A fixed timetable limits your abilities to learn more skills, both professional and personal, while you are working on a job. A flexible timetable makes the person bound to the business and takes away a chance at personal growth. I believe that a middle ground should be struck on both sides where flexible and fixed times are achieved by both employers and businessmen alike. Employees should evaluate their lifestyle and see which of these two makes the most sense and focus on that as an objective. The wrong choice can be devastating.

Fixed and Variable Income: Fixed income is beneficial in jobs because the person earning a certain amount, can depend on a timely paycheck. Variable income is preferred in a business with a prospect of growth and a profit that will be passed on to the business owner and employees. Fixed income has a shortcoming in that the employee has tied up all of his effort in the job. Variable income has a problem in that businessman is tied to his business financially, in a *sink or swim* environment. The solution is for an employee to also have a bit of entrepreneurial spirit and serve the businessman by cultivating a business, which provides stable profits every quarter, significant growth, and yields financial rewards for them and the team.

Job Creators Vs. Job Seekers: The employee is the job seeker, so the market that matches their experience or education is his *oyster*. While the businessman gives the jobs to the applicants that fit the company's needs, without knowing the outcome for certain, but sharing an opportunity for a safe future and positive financial rewards. The employee will be temporarily be locked out of the job options available in the market and rely on the businessman to serve as the job provider. Either of these actions will be fulfilled and come with their own set of limitations.

Stability and Reliability: Jobs serve as a source of stability in a person's life, as the person is able to develop plans and rely on financial resources. Private businesses are reliable, in one way, because you can never be fired from your own company. But the stability that comes with owning your own business is tenuous at best. It is always open to potential threats they may have great impact. The unreliability of owning a business is also the uncertainty of the challenges that can create significant costs the owner. Employment decisions are the delicate balance between taking on the cause by yourself or tackling it as part of a larger organization.

Skills Development: Skill development occurs in different ways, in both employment and business ownership. Business ownership gives one experience and a strong awareness of decision making, while employment helps you develop technical skills and keep up with the market's standards in your chosen field. Employment allows for the sharing of training and development provided by the employer. The school of *hard knocks* is the teacher of record for small business owners.

Quality of Life: The quality of life for both employees and business owners depends on the extent of their financial capability. If you are trained in a high-paying field, then you will earn considerable financial gains, and will have a quality of life accordingly. The business owner also has the potential to become successful and gain the same quality of life by using their own skills and capabilities, driving success from within their own organization. This again is dependent on the choices you make.

Mind Set of Employee and Employer: The mindset of the employee and employer varies from company to company. An employee can find himself working with a very challenging boss, they wish they could replace. The employer may find themselves working with an employee who is crucial to his business, but hard to work with. These factors are fluid and can change in an instance without question. All requiring the team members to adjust as necessary, in order to achieve success.

Benefit for Future Generations: The future generation may benefit far more from an entrepreneur workplace, where many options become available. Seeing likeminded individuals conduct their businesses, often pushes them to do the same, becoming more independent in their thought process.

The individuals psychological makeup of an entrepreneur is a bit of a mystery. Most individuals think that the entrepreneur is a unique mind, only born once in a generation. We believe that Bill Gates, Warren Buffet, and Mark Zuckerberg bear the fruit of a once in a lifetime mind. But the truth is that a successful entrepreneur is a surprisingly open person about what the trade is about. The next chapter might tackle a few of those perceptions, press on.

Something to Remember:
It is critical to believe that trust among your employees will build your organization

Chapter 16
Live to Learn:
Develop an Entrepreneurial Mindset

"Live every day like it is your last and learn everyday like you will live forever" - Mahatma Gandhi

A businessperson is an entrepreneur for life. An entrepreneurial mindset is the key to launching your new venture and gaining the correct results—be it world domination or fixing a problem. Lots of people look in awe from the sidelines and see entrepreneurs as the people who make things happen. As mentioned before, many people find the psychological makeup of an entrepreneur to be a mystery.

It is thought provoking to listen to the advice of entrepreneurs. Below I have listed nine successful entrepreneurs, which may provide some clarity regarding the practical side of the entrepreneurship mindset. These are not simply the big names but the real ones.

Their advice is important because it comes—not from theory—but practice—and right from the source. You might even see tips from the co-founders, whose products you use daily.

Entrepreneurship Mindset- Sean Rad

Sean Rad is the Co-Founder of Tinder, the location-based dating app, took a while to get where it is today. The idea for Tinder was highly niche specific and took up considerable time to get the right traction with the target audience. Here is the advice of Sean Rad for those who face a similar dilemma with their niche startup that has not taken off.

"When you are building a startup, it's difficult. Particularly, a startup that is expanding at the rate of Tinder. You must give the effort 100% of your time and you must be committed. Solving the problem has to be personal or else you're going to disintegrate."

The advice seems simple, but it has profound ramifications. If a person is building a niche startup that caters to a specific audience, they must understand that overnight success is not an option. They will work for half a decade or more anonymously before the masses will embrace their product. They must also be prepared to invest a considerable amount of time before it becomes a successful investment. This time must be spent with perseverance and focus on maintaining its best possible shape. If the business is ill-equipped even before its launch, it will never reach its full potential.

Entrepreneurship Mindset - Subroto Bagchi

The Co-Founder of Mind Tree, the most successful digital marketing agency in India, with a revenue of one billion dollars yearly, has a unique insight into the act of entrepreneurship. "Selling is not a pushy, winner-takes-all, macho act. It is an empathy-led, process-driven, and knowledge-intensive discipline. Because, in the end, people buy from people."

This is the backbone of launching a successful entrepreneurial venture, as most individuals believe that sales revenue is entirely dependent on personal persuasion in the early days of a business.

In modern times, a client is a person who comes to the seller with standardized aims that need to be achieved. The idea of knowing how to make the sales has greatly transitioned in favor of big data, data analytics, and other tools of calibration. The modern entrepreneur needs numbers and active knowledge in his niche. He needs to show his investor that he is the most knowledgeable person in the trade and retains the most intelligent employees and customer based on talent, quality, and expertise.

Entrepreneurship Mindset - Jules Pieri

Failures among entrepreneurs is actually a commonality. Unique examples are the Founders of Twitter and LinkedIn, until they gained exceptional success. Then, there is the age-old tale of J.K. Rowling. A single mother who was on welfare checks with a manuscript that was rejected by 12 publishers. And then The-Boy-Who-Lived met every teenager in the world, and the rest is history

Now, let us look at Jules Pieri, founder of Grommet, an e-commerce platform specializing in unique gifts and products that are not usually available online. The startup is fast rising and has made its mark quite early in the game. Here is what Jules has to say about the journey of a startup.

"Ignore the hype of the startups that you see in the press. Mostly, it's a pack of lies. Half of these startups will be dead in a year. So, focus on building your business so you can be the one left standing."

The truth is that before gaining success in a startup, the business team needs time to strengthen the business at its core. Building a business is like constructing a building. If the infrastructure, the workforce management, and the operating model are not thoroughly developed, the end product will fail. Let's look at some other examples.

Entrepreneurship Mindset - Barnaby Lashbrook

When it comes to investment needs for a new venture, most entrepreneurs think big bucks mean big success. If a startup has a strong stream of revenue lined up, they will have an easier time understanding and investing in their product, infrastructure, and operations. Even though a primary and robust stream of revenue is key to a successful venture, it is most often just wishful thinking. There are some lessons to be learned from those who have succeeded, but it is critical to internalize that funding, which is often the most challenging and NEVER EASY.

Let's look at Barnaby Lashbrook, the founder of Times-Enterprise, who had something to say on the matter. "Don't assume that borrowing lots of money can make your startup fly. There are many things to the business other than investors, and it's possible to succeed with your startup without breaking the bank."

So, the lesson is not that running up a bunch of debt can ensure success. Utilizing the proceeds of that activity to drive the business success is critical as you will not have a steady stream of investors if your great idea cannot achieve profitability. The businesses that thrive today have a strong sense of long-term planning with a sense of spontaneity necessary to solve the unexpected issues that continuously crop up in every startup venture.

Entrepreneurship Mindset - Andy Groove

The prior narrative provided some sensible advice that any start-up leadership can find support. Enough with the sensible advice for a minute. Here are genuinely whacky strategies from the tech gurus of this generation.

Andy Grooves is the former CEO of Intel and a truly well-respected name in the tech industry.

He says, "Only the paranoid survives." This one-liner is the best advice on entrepreneurship ventures that one can receive. In a newly founded venture, everything can go wrong, whilst we always remember that It's Never So Bad That It Can't Get Worse. The best way to manage a colossal set of unfortunate events raining down on your precious venture—is to develop a sense of fully-developed paranoia.

Even though paranoia would seem, at first, to have a negative connotation, it represents the idea that every possible calamity should be kept in mind, especially while launching a business. Prepare to be ready when things do go wrong.

Entrepreneurship Mindset - Melanie Perkins

Melanie is the Co-Founder of Canva, a highly successful graphic designing website that quickly gained a place at the front of the line in graphic design. No discussion on entrepreneurial ventures should be complete without discussing the significance of the strategy behind a free product. Many entrepreneurs seek market penetration rates and customer acceptance, as they often find themself giving away a product for free to encourage customer sampling.

It is a highly debated topic in the entrepreneurial world, whether it is a good idea to provide free services. The argument for free services comes from Facebook and Google examples, as they provide free services and yet gain exemplary revenue from advertisement. The counter argument comes from companies that are not tech giants, their products are not online services. The products they develop are expensive and cannot be given away for free. Profitability cannot be achieved as the company continues to sacrifice revenue for product acceptance. Here is what Melanie thinks about the topic; "If you can offer a free tier that provides a lot of value, it will naturally help your product to spread to the potential market more rapidly." Here, Melanie has shown a unique way out of the dilemma. Once mass adoption becomes a reality among prospective customers, it is also potentially beneficial to give a less expensive product out for free, necessitating that the team develop smaller and cheaper products to be made available for sampling and testing. In this way, the company is not encouraging unhealthy pricing practices, yet gaining valuable customer exposure and user conversancy with the product.

Entrepreneurship Mindset - Brian Chesky

It seems obvious that the desire to invent the next big thing runs freely within the veins of every entrepreneur. They all want to develop an extremely lucrative idea, change the world, and make millions of dollars. The truth, however, is the innovation does NOT always drive the company success. Certainly, innovation gains considerable interest among the investor class, but the long-term success of any innovative company is the ability to succeed in the foundational actions necessary to drive the BUSINESS success, not just the product success. Innovation, often times, has little to do with ultimate success as an entrepreneur in real life.

The real entrepreneur may find himself in situations where his business expertise is far more essential than his invention. The founder of Airbnb, Brian Chesky, insists that innovation is not necessarily significant for all entrepreneurs. "If we tried to think of a good idea, we probably wouldn't have been able to think of a good idea. You often develop innovative ideas and products as you seek to find the solutions to a problem and/or opportunity in your own life."

As Brian so astutely observes, problem-solving is the most necessary form of innovation that a person can exhibit; if a person can develop a fluid model and cater to his consumers while troubleshooting the obstacles along the way, then voila-success! Frequently this is the only requirement that he must fulfill!

Entrepreneurship Mindset - Ryan Holmes

Hootsuite is an example of the modern innovation model. Hootsuite focuses on delivering social media management platforms to digital marketers and is a highly successful venture with 15 million users worldwide. This particular venture is unusual, as the founder provided interesting advice regarding initial funding. Who would imagine that Hootsuite's founder relied on bootstrapping his business in the early years, instead of looking for an investor? His thoughts seem remarkably simple: "When in doubt, bootstrap. Using your own personal resources is the easiest way to start a business. You don't have to convince investors about the merits of your idea. You just have to convince yourself and your friends." Save the investor pitches until you have achieved some level of success and the valuations will be much more beneficial to your early angels.

The fact that Ryan considered bootstrapping a viable alternative to finding investors should be an exciting thought for entrepreneurs who have a great idea that needs vetting. It should be noted that some of the most successful ventures of our generation, such as Google and Facebook, were launched through bootstrapping. Mark Zuckerberg (very famously!) wrote the code for Facebook on the windows of his Harvard University dorm room. The basic model of Google was launched at Stanford University by two Ph.D. candidates at the university. Last but not least, J. K. Rowling wrote Harry Potter while collecting welfare checks! The world is riddled with similar stories where the guts to try and a belief in a pioneering spirit can conquer the world!

Entrepreneurship Mindset - Dennis Crowley

The Co-founder of FourSquare provides another interesting strategy on entrepreneurship. The credo involves the requirement that the founder never outright lie to his investors, but also should never share the best-case scenario as a part of your business plan. Dennis thinks that a lot can go wrong with an investment. But if the investors are aware of the worst-case scenario and are willing to stay in the boat, even in the worst times, then they will remain loyal supporters.

"We learned many things while building FourSquare. One of the most important lessons is to be clear to investors about what the company will and will not do. And be open about the priorities of the things that have to be done." As Dennis stated, the best option for a company is always providing an understanding of the worst-case scenario so that the investors never feel blindsided if they end up down that dark alley.

These are just some examples of the inspiring entrepreneurship mindset and the different perspectives of some of today's brightest minds. Master these strategies so that you can toil through the thick and thin of the coming day, weeks, and months ahead. You will only be as good as your ability to work through the challenges, as you build a healthy bone to survive the worst that may come your way.

Something to Remember:

Building a business is like constructing a building. If the infrastructure, workforce management, and operating model are not thoroughly developed, the end product will disappoint.

Chapter 17
Putting it All Together
Ok, so now what do I do?

"Don't judge each day by the harvest you reap but by the seeds that you plant." -Robert Louis Stephenson

Great things happen as we navigate through this thing called "life." From these chapters, I hope you have discovered that almost anything and everything is achievable. But it will depend largely on what you plan for, commit to, and want to achieve. Many of the tips and lessons learned are things you already know, or maybe they will be simple reminders. Most importantly, remember people are naturally drawn to others who have a positive attitude and are grateful…thank everybody that deserves it!

Discovering one day that, *oh no I'm in charge* solidifies that your work is being rewarded…even if it doesn't feel like it right away! This can truly impact the things you accomplish, both at work and in your personal life. Surely managing your own GSI can have a dramatic impact on you and your team, and will provide the energy to succeed. Find similarly inclined people to share the ride on your journey. Not only will this association be beneficial to your career, and make your days more pleasurable, it will also aid you in impacting the lives of others, who may be completely unrelated to your workplace.

I encourage you to go back and reread these chapters, at least the chapter heading, and notable quotes. If they can help to reinforce the things that will matter most to you and your success, then you will have invested your time wisely. If at first, they are unclear, read them over again. and apply the strategies in areas that most closely match the skills and attributes you aspire to, whether you are the learner or the leader.

That is part of the work and part of the fun.

Thanks for sharing this journey with me. I wish you nothing but great success!

Acknowledgements

The simplest acknowledgement I can offer is to recognize all those with whom I have shared the business and academic world. Each of those team members provided me with thought provoking challenges, insight, and support so that, together, we could accomplish great things, and learn along the way.

I also offer my humblest appreciation to acclaimed novelist Sally Fernandez who has provided inspiration and support throughout this process.

About the Author

Dr. Gary B. Vonk is a lifelong learner who has been working his way through life as a student and leader. He has held various retail and corporate positions with increasing degrees of responsibility.

His work has taken him through many of the major cities in California and throughout the West.

He has also spent many years working in corporate America in positions ranging from Director of Customer Service and Vice President of Operations to COO, President and CEO.

He has worked in small organizations with narrow customer focus as well as international companies with locations in twenty countries.

All the while he has sought to develop an environment where success is a product of a team with mutual goals. Whether it is simply to get through the day, or get through the next Board meeting. The goals have always been to use the 'people power' to tackle the problems we face and create a team of learners and leaders who will continue to build the company.

Dr. Vonk has often said, "As the leader, I really don't want my phone to ring, as I know I have people in place who get the work done."

His goal is to put responsibility in the hands of those who have earned it!